**TEACH Y**

CW01064745

Lotus 1-2-3
for Windows

Release 5

David Royall

Hodder & Stoughton

A MEMBER OF THE HODDER HEADLINE GROUP

A catalogue record for this title is available from the British Library.

ISBN 0 340 65492 9 (Book only)
ISBN 0 340 65493 7 (Book/disc pack)

First published 1996
Impression number 10 9 8 7 6 5 4 3 2
Year   1999 1998 1997

Typeset by Transet Limited, Coventry, England.
Printed in Great Britain for Hodder & Stoughton Educational, a division of Hodder
Headline Plc, 338 Euston Road, London NW1 3BH by Cox & Wyman Ltd, Reading,
Berkshire.

CONTENTS

INTRODUCTION

Teach Yourself Lotus 1-2-3 for Windows is an introductory guide for anyone learning how to use the Lotus 1-2-3 spreadsheet package for the first time. It is ideal for people who know little or nothing about computers or spreadsheets as well as those who are familiar with both but want to learn how to use this Windows-based spreadsheet.

Teach Yourself Lotus 1-2-3 for Windows:

- Takes readers through simple step-by-step practical activities.
- Explains the underlying principles behind what is happening.
- Contains numerous illustrations throughout showing what users can expect to see on their screen as they work through the package.
- Encourages good spreadsheet practice while conforming to the Windows style of performing actions.
- Contains comprehensive references that will prove invaluable once the basic skills have been learnt.
- Contains many exercises offering suggestions as to how to apply spreadsheets as well as serving as a way of developing your spreadsheet skills.

You should work through the book from start to finish as each chapter builds on the lessons learnt in previous chapters.

The book is illustrated with screen dumps from Lotus 1-2-3 for Windows Release 5. Those readers using Release 1 or Release 4 can also get the full benefit of the book because guidance is given where Release 5 differs in operation from previous releases.

1
GETTING STARTED

1.1 Aims of this chapter

This chapter gives an outline of what the Lotus 1-2-3 for Windows spreadsheet is, what it can do and how you should prepare your computer for its use. There is also an explanation of some computer terminology that may be new to you. It will help you get started and ensure that you have what is needed to be successful in using this Lotus product.

1.2 What is a spreadsheet?

A spreadsheet is the electronic equivalent of an accountant's ledger: a large piece of paper divided by vertical columns and horizontal rows into a grid of cells. The name derives from the spreading of the organisation's accounts on a sheet of paper. On a computer the user can directly enter numbers, formulae or text into the cells.

Screen dump 1.1 shows what an empty spreadsheet might look like. The top part of the screen holds various menus and icons that will be used throughout the work you do. The spreadsheet is headed [Untitled] and the spreadsheet working area is made up of a grid of lines on a white background. Your opening spreadsheet screen may differ from this if you are using a different version of the package or the package was installed on your machine differently.

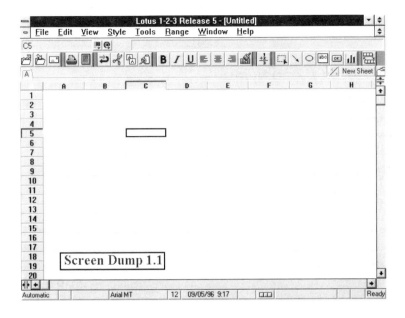

Screen Dump 1.1

There are letters along the top of the columns and numbers in rows down the left side of the spreadsheet working area. The small oblong in the middle of the blank area which is outlined in black is referred to as a cell. Each cell is identified by its co-ordinates, like a map reference or point on a graph. The highlighted section here is at C5, i.e., *column* C and *row* 5.

Use your mouse to move from cell to cell.

Click on cell B1, type a number (e.g. 4) and press the **Enter** key. Click on cell C1, type a number (e.g. 6) and press the **Enter** key. Then click on A1 and type =B1*C1. A1 displays the number you typed in cell B1 multiplied by the number you typed in cell C1. Type a different number in cell B1 or C1 and press the **Enter** Key. The number displayed in cell A1 will automatically change.

Note that you need to precede a formula (=B1*C1 is a formula) with = or +.

The spreadsheet effectively becomes a screen-based calculator capable of being printed or displayed as a graph.

As a 'tool', accountancy is by no means the only work for which spreadsheets can be used. Some examples of the power of spreadsheets are:

1 What if? analysis

Any figure can be changed at any time and the new results will automatically be shown. Thus a What if? analysis might be: what if sales were to increase by 10%? The spreadsheet can calculate this easily. This facility of being able to recalculate formulae quickly makes spreadsheets powerful, useful and popular analytical tools.

2 Goal seeking

Some spreadsheets are used in order to seek goals. For example, a spreadsheet can be set up showing sales and costs in a business and become a model that can determine at what price profits will be maximised.

3 Graphing

In this instance, the spreadsheet is used to represent tables and figures in the form of graphs.

4 Storing records of information

A spreadsheet can be used to hold records of information such as details of costs accumulated for a specific job. Such information can be altered quickly and can be used as the basis of a contract tender or for price determination. This type of application is often referred to as database management. Using the Lotus 1-2-3 spreadsheet as a database manager will be covered in this book.

In practice, spreadsheets will be used for a combination of the above. Spreadsheets are flexible modelling tools which can be readily adapted for many jobs involving repetitive numerical calculations.

Other examples of their use:

● Financial plans and budgets can be represented as a table, with columns for time periods (e.g. months) and rows for different elements of the plan (e.g. costs and revenue).

- Tax, investment and loan calculations.
- Statistics can be displayed, such as averages, standard deviations, time series and regression analysis. Many in-built statistical functions are available in Lotus 1-2-3 for Windows.
- Merging branch or departmental accounts to form group (or consolidated) accounts. This involves merging two or more spreadsheets together.
- Currency conversion – useful for an organisation with overseas interests.
- Timetabling and roster planning of staff within organisations or departments.
- In an educational establishment – the recording of class lists, attendance, student marks.

You will probably think of many more potential applications as you work through the book.

Lotus 1-2-3 for Windows is a product developed by a company called Lotus Corporation and incorporates three standard applications of spreadsheet, database and graphics. You will soon appreciate that the uses of spreadsheets often combines these three applications.

—— 1.3 Hardware and software ——

Hardware refers to the physical components of a computer system, while software refers to the programs that are used to give instructions to the computer. Both are needed if the computer is to achieve anything at all.

Software for a computer will come in many forms; essentially there will be an operating system which will come with the computer system, and applications software which you normally buy as extra. Lotus 1-2-3 for Windows is an example of applications software. This product operates in the Windows environment, so you will also need Microsoft Windows software, which is an extra application used with an operating system.

When the machine is switched on, the computer will need some instructions about how to operate the computer system, hence the term operating system. Different computers will have varying kinds of operating systems, which needs to be considered when you are buying applications.

When choosing hardware, you will need to make decisions on such issues as how much disk space you will need and the quality of your printer. When selecting software, you are making decisions about what you want your computer to do for you.

1.4 Computer needs

It is important to bear in mind that some older PCs will not be able to run Lotus 1-2-3 for Windows because they will not have sufficient memory (RAM) to run both Windows and Lotus 1-2-3. Always check the System Requirements with your software dealer.

1.5 Operating systems

Although all computers appear similar from the outside, they may well have different operating systems. An operating system is the language that any particular machine has to work with, in much the same way that different peoples of the world communicate in different languages.

Most microcomputers use the operating system MS-DOS (Microsoft Disk Operating System). However there are different versions of MS-DOS. The different versions have come about because computers have advanced over the years with new and more powerful devices, and changes in the operating systems have been required for the new devices to be operated.

Increasingly the operating system OS/2 (Operating System 2) is being used. This has the added advantage over MS-DOS in that many 'jobs' can be executed at the same time. For example, while the computer is printing, an operator can get on with something else without any slow-down in speed. Alternatively, it will give operators the facility of being able to work on a number of different packages at the same time from one machine.

Computers that are linked together, or 'networked' – in an office, for example, require a different operating system again, because there will be a number of different machines all working from a common system (normally called a file server). The network operating system will, for example, need to administer all machines using the same software package and a single printer.

With such a range of systems, it is important that before you buy a copy of Lotus 1-2-3 for Windows, you check with your supplier that the version of Lotus 1-2-3 for Windows you are purchasing matches the machine and operating system you are intending to use it with.

—————— 1.6 Processor types ——————

Part of the computer's hardware is called the processor. All computers need such processing devices as they form the main attributes of a computer system. Over the last few years such processors have become more sophisticated and more powerful.

Not all software packages will run on all processors; so, again, you need to be careful that the software purchased is correct for the machine you have. It is not for a book like this to discuss the varying processor types nor is it necessary for you to know all about them in order to be able to take full advantage of this spreadsheet package. However, you will need to know what kind of processor you have if you are going to purchase software. Most dealers will be able to identify this by the model of machine you have.

—————— 1.7 Disk drives ——————

You will normally find three types of disk drive in your PC – a floppy disk drive and a hard disk drive and, nowadays, a CD Rom.

The hard disk is usually pre-installed and formatted. It is capable of holding very large volumes of data and you install the software which is used to manipulate the data on to the hard disk.

A floppy disk drive is used to store data on removable small 3.5 inch disks. When you buy software, it sometimes comes on such floppy disks. Clear and easy to follow instructions on how to install the software on to the hard disk will come with the software. Floppy disk drives are also used for backing up files as a precaution against loss of data.

New PCs now have a third disk drive – the CD Rom. Because software is now very complicated it is easier to install from a CD Rom than from, say, 20 floppy disks.

Older computers may have only as little hard disk storage as 60 megabytes. Floppy disks normally store 1.4 megabytes. This may not be enough for some software.

It is often difficult to appreciate what a megabyte of data actually is, but to give you some idea, a book of this size, if converted to computer data, would fit on to a 1.4 megabyte disk.

1.8 Screen types

Many portable and notebook computers will only have a monochrome display, but a colour screen is easier to use and makes presentations more impressive.

All new machines will have full graphics capabilities. Older computers will vary in their ability to display graphics. Lotus 1-2-3 for Windows requires graphics capabilities to operate.

1.9 Printers

You will almost certainly want to print out your spreadsheet and graphs. Not all printers will necessarily be able to do this. Printers will vary in speed of print, quality of print and paper width (printers are usually 80-column or 132-column width).

Here is a list of the main types of printer available and a brief description of what they can achieve.

Ink Jet printers. These offer good quality at a low cost. Colour ink jet printers have now become cheaper and are an attractive option.

Dot Matrix. These are in common use, with colour options, but are being replaced by ink jet printers for low budget users. A 24-pin printer will print with greater definition than a 9-pin printer. Matrix printers will also produce graphics output.

Laser printers. These give the best output. They work rather like a photocopier, and can produce camera ready copy for publishing. However, laser printers are the most expensive option.

Any Windows compatible printer will print your Lotus 1-2-3 files and graphics.

—— 1.10 The keyboard and mouse ——

Most keyboards are fairly standard. Before starting, examine your keyboard to determine the whereabouts of the following:

Number pads. On most keyboards there are two sets of number keys from 0 to 9; one set above the QWERTY letters and the other as a number pad to the right-hand side of the keyboard. The reason for this is that some users prefer to use the number pad to the right of the keyboard in the same way they would use a standard calculator. If you do decide to use the number pad, you will need to set the Num Lock 'on' when doing so.

Function Keys. These are specially programmed to perform certain functions. On most keyboards the function keys are either along the top or grouped together on the left-hand side of the keyboard. Each key is normally numbered F1, F2, F3, etc. You will, in time, find some of these very useful when using the Lotus 1-2-3 package.

Insert, Home, Page Up, Page Down, Delete, End. These are found on most keyboards and, along with the function keys, offer ways of taking shortcuts. These keys will perform different functions depending upon the package in use. Lotus 1-2-3 for Windows makes full use of these keys.

Arrow keys. These often appear as separate function keys on keyboards. If they do not, then you will have to use the ones that appear on the number pad.

* (multiplication). This appears above the number 8 key near the top of your keyboard. It is used in order to avoid confusion with the conventional symbol for multiplication, x . / (forward slash) is used for division. So, 8*4 means 8 multiplied by 4; 8/4 means 8 divided by 4.

Ctrl (Control). This will always be used in conjunction with another key. For example, holding down the Ctrl key and pressing the character C (referred to as **Ctrl**+C) is used in the Windows environment for copying information.

Alt. This is used in a similar way to the **Ctrl** key in that it is pressed simultaneously with other keys to provide a variety of other facilities. For example, holding down the Alt key and pressing the F4 function key (Alt+F4) is used to quit Lotus 1-2-3 for Windows.

Esc (Escape). This key operates rather like a function key and is often used, as is the case in Lotus 1-2-3 for Windows, to 'back track' on a sequence of events or 'undo' an activity.

~ (tilde). This is a special key used for the more advanced features of Lotus 1-2-3. It is worth checking its whereabouts on your keyboard.

PrtScr (Print Screen). This allows you to 'dump' a copy of the screen to your printer or to the Clipboard. The Clipboard is a part of your computer's internal memory that can be recalled at a later stage.

Remember to distinguish / (forward slash) from the \ (back slash). The forward slash is used as a division symbol in most applications.

Getting to know your keyboard is important. However, you will find that if you are new to computing this will take quite some time and you will need to be patient. Progress can be slow when you are learning a new package such as Lotus 1-2-3 for Windows and discovering your keyboard at the same time.

Computers now come equipped with a pointing device called a mouse, which offers an alternative to the keyboard for performing actions. The mouse is moved around on a flat surface, often on a mouse mat, and interacts with a small cursor that appears on the screen. The cursor acts as a pointer and can be positioned on an icon on the screen so that when the mouse is 'clicked', by pressing the left-hand button, a selected action is activated.

As is the case with all Windows software, the Lotus package has been particularly developed for you to make full use of the mouse. With practice, the mouse will offer many shortcuts over entering commands via a keyboard.

——— 1.11 Data storage on disk ———

The data stored on hard or floppy disks has to be organised in a way that can be understood by both the user and the computer. Data will be collected and stored in files.

For now it is simply good enough to know what kind of files data is organised into. There are three types of file that Lotus 1-2-3 users need to be know about:

1 Operating System files contain the software that the computer needs to instruct it how to work. These files will appear on the hard disk before the Lotus 1-2-3 package is ever introduced.

2 Applications software files will be large in number and the process of placing such files on to the hard disk is called installing the software.

3 Data keyed in by the user will be placed in one of the application directories. For each spreadsheet, for example, there will be a file with its own name, chosen by the user.

Disks, both hard and floppy, have a root directory which acts as a starting-point from which sub-directories are created, and into which, files are stored.

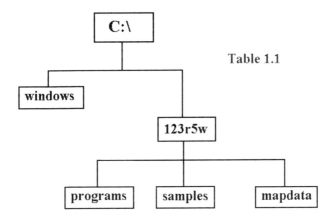

Table 1.1

In **Table 1.1** it can be seen that the root directory C: contains two sub-directories: Windows and 123r5w. Lotus files are stored in the 123r5w sub-directory. However, you can move them to a further 'samples' directory if you wish. Organising files in directories is part of the process of file management. In many ways, it is no different from organising files in a filing cabinet. The art of good file management is one of knowing where to find information quickly and efficiently.

—— 1.12 Computer memory ——

Computer memory is the memory which exists inside the computer other than on disk. Some computer memory is required to store programs needed to control the computer system - the Operating System. Much more memory is needed for two other main purposes:

1 To hold the application software when it is in use. Lotus 1-2-3 for Windows is a large software package made up of a great number of separate files all stored on hard disk. Not all of the package is loaded into memory at any one time; this is done only when it is needed. Lotus will frequently load files into memory to instruct it what to do in certain circumstances, and then dispose of this from memory when it is no longer required.

2 To hold data generated by the package itself. Again, not all data generated will need to be held in memory at any one time; it will be stored in many separate files and saved on disk.

The size of your computer memory (Random Access Memory, or RAM) is limited. Interacting with files stored on disk allows a computer to extend its capabilities considerably. It is important that when buying software you make sure your machine has enough memory in the computer itself to cope with the version of Lotus 1-2-3 for Windows you are buying. This is especially important when buying any package for Windows. Release 5 for Windows requires a minimum of 4 megabytes of RAM (8 megabytes for some of the more advanced features).

The more RAM your computer has, the better.

—— 1.13 Menus ——

You will often come across the term 'menu' when working with computers. A menu is simply a list of options that you can choose from. Quite often when selecting a menu option you are given yet more options from that option – a sub-menu. This hierarchical structure of menus is now very common among applications on computers. In practice, the successful use of computer software often largely rests with the operator knowing the way around a set of menus.

A good deal of your effort in teaching yourself Lotus 1-2-3 for Windows will consist of finding your way around the Lotus 1-2-3 menu structure. Lotus 1-2-3 also has a large collection of SmartIcons that are used to bypass the menu structure and can be used to speed up many activities. The main emphasis throughout this book, however, is to become as familiar as possible with the menu structure of Lotus 1-2-3 for Windows.

1.14 Installing Lotus 1-2-3 for Windows

When your software arrives you will receive:

- A number of floppy disks containing your software
- Documentation that will contain:

  Instructions on setting up Lotus 1-2-3 for Windows for
     your computer
  Software registration card
  A manual
  A tutorial.

If your hard disk has been prepared in the correct way then the whole process of installing Lotus on to a hard disk has been made a little easier by Lotus, as they supply an installation program on one of the floppy disks. What the installation program will achieve is to place the required files on to your hard disk in the correct directories. It will also create the program icon in part of the Windows screen, giving you easy access to the program.

Assuming you have a hard disk system or are using a network, then to install the software all you need to do is:

- Switch your computer on and make sure Windows is running.
- Place the disk marked **installation** into your floppy disk drive. If you have two drives, then it should go into the one your system refers to as A: drive.
- Using your mouse select the **File** menu from the Program Manager window. Click on **Run** and type in A:INSTALL.EXE in the **Command Line** box. **Screen dump 1.2** shows what you should type.

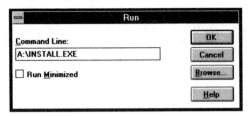

Screen Dump 1.2

● When the Command Line has been entered, click on **OK** to start the installation program running.

After a few moments, when the program has examined your computer, a dialogue box will appear on your screen. **Screen dump 1.3** shows such a dialogue which requires a response from you before you can start.

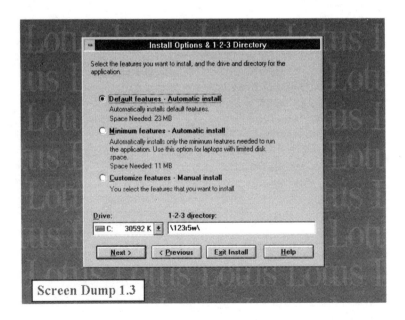

Screen Dump 1.3

First you must decide how much of the Lotus program you want installed. If you are limited for hard disk space, then select the **Minimum features – Automatic install**, otherwise accept the **Default features – Automatic install**. Choosing the **Customize** option will require you to work through some more dialogue boxes deciding on exactly what you want installed. The Drive panel informs you of the available space you have on your disk. The **1-2-3 directory** panel is the directory where Lotus 1-2-3 will be installed; this can be altered if you wish.

Once satisfied with the settings in this dialogue box, click on **Next** to carry on with installation.

A set of instructions will appear on the screen guiding you through the rest of installation procedures. When a package like Lotus 1-2-3 for Windows is purchased it is sold on the understanding that the software is for the use of the organisation or person who purchased it, and you will be required to type in such details. This forms part of the opening screen when the package is loaded.

Follow the instructions as they appear; they are largely self explanatory. You will need to have all the other disks at hand. Each disk will be asked for in turn via a dialogue box similar to the one shown in **Screen dump 1.4**. This requires you to change disk and then click on **OK**.

Screen Dump 1.4

Eventually you will leave the installation program and will find yourself back at the original window with the new Lotus 1-2-3 for Windows icon appearing and it will be ready for you to run.

If you have installed the software incorrectly, then you can always reinstall it. To do this you can run the install program again in exactly the same way as you did before. If you re-run install or wish to make alterations to the way you installed the package in the first instance, you may not need to use all the disks again.

——— 1.15 Getting started ———

With the diversity of operating systems and the different versions of Lotus 1-2-3, it is very difficult to give precise instructions about installing the package in a book like this. However, once installed, the rest is a little more straightforward. **Screen dump 1.5** shows how a set of program icons have been created and placed into a group window. Again, this might vary according to the version of Lotus 1-2-3 you are using and how it was installed.

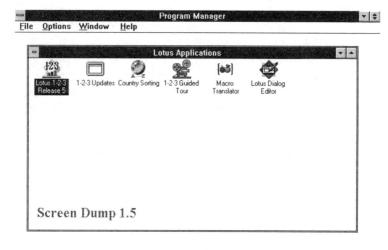

Screen Dump 1.5

To get into Lotus 1-2-3 for Windows simply position the pointer on the icon labelled **Lotus 1-2-3** (Highlighted in **Screen dump 1.5**) with your mouse and perform a double click with the mouse to activate the program. There will be a delay while the spreadsheet is loading. After this short delay the program will start with a blank spreadsheet. If you are a Release 5 user, then a preliminary dialogue box will appear. Click on the **Cancel** button that appears inside it.

The empty spreadsheet you start with will look something like the one in **Screen dump 1.1**.

If you are working on a network system then the whole approach to loading Lotus 1-2-3 for Windows may be very different in that an opening screen may appear from which you select the Lotus package. Before progressing to the next chapter you are strongly advised to familiarise yourself with how to enter your particular set up of Lotus 1-2-3 for Windows, as variations on how to get started can be quite considerable.

1.16 Chapter summary

In this chapter you have covered the following points:

- what a spreadsheet is and what it can do.
- what software is and what hardware is needed to run Lotus 1-2-3 for Windows.
- the way data are stored in files and how directories are used to store files.
- how a hierarchical directory structure can be used to manage the file storage on a disk.
- how to install Lotus 1-2-3 for Windows on to a hard disk and subsequently how to get started with the Lotus package.

2

THE BASICS OF
SPREADSHEETS

2.1 Aims of this chapter

The aim of this chapter is to help you get some idea of what a spread-sheet does and its style of operation. Most activities will be illustrated by examples which will show you the capabilities of the Lotus package.

To begin with, it is assumed that you have installed your version of Lotus 1-2-3 for Windows on to your machine. If you have not done so, then refer to the sections in Chapter 1 on installing Lotus 1-2-3 for Windows .

2.2 Getting started

- Switch on your machine and wait for either a DOS prompt or for Windows to load.
- If Windows has not automatically loaded, then type WIN and press the Enter key. Lotus 1-2-3 for Windows will only load and run when Windows is running.
- Highlight the Lotus 1-2-3 icon with your mouse and double click the left button.

If you are a Release 5 user, then a dialogue box will appear headed Welcome to 1-2-3. The use of this dialogue box will be shown at the end of this chapter. If such a dialogue box has appeared, click on the Cancel button to clear it from your screen.

At this stage you should see a blank spreadsheet similar to the one in **Screen dump 2.1** with cell location A1 highlighted.

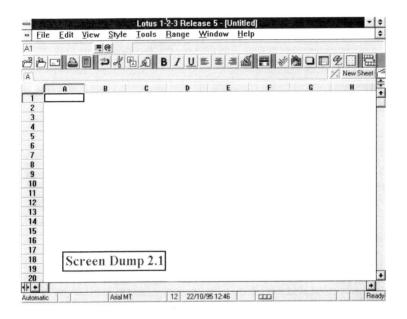

Screen Dump 2.1

The control panel

The top five lines form the control panel. The top line is the title and reads Lotus 1-2-3 Release 5 - [Untitled] . On the right side are two square boxes containing the minimise and maximise buttons to reduce the screen to an icon, and to fill the screen, respectively. **Screen dump 2.1** has been maximised.

The second line is the main menu bar:

File   Edit   View   Style   Tools   Range   Window   Help

This menu will allow you to perform a whole host of actions which you will work with through this book. To the right of this bar appears a square control button which can be used to put the Release 5 sheet in a window. It is worth experimenting with this as it can be used to get the same appearance that is illustrated in the screen dumps.

The third line is called the Edit bar and is largely clear. The edit line will guide you when entering data and formulae into your spreadsheet. Each option shown on the edit line has a letter underlined. This indicates the character that can be used with the *Alt* key on your keyboard, and is an alternative to using the mouse; i.e. press *Alt* followed by the character underlined rather than clicking on the option with your mouse.

The fourth line shows a row of SmartIcons which are used to make time-saving short cuts. They are all customisable so that you can display icons that relate to actions that you use most often. Release 5 users have the benefit of a small balloon containing a brief description of the function of an icon which appears when the mouse pointer is on the icon.

A further line will also appear that indicates which spreadsheet you are using – the worksheet tab. At present it shows you are in spreadsheet A. The rest of the screen will contain the spreadsheet itself.

To the right of the worksheet work area is a bar that has two splitter boxes. These will be demonstrated later. There is also a vertical scroll bar which will be used when your spreadsheet becomes too large for the screen to show it all at any one time.

At the bottom of the worksheet work area appears another bar with a horizontal scroll arrow which will be used in much the same way as the vertical scroll – to let you see parts of the spreadsheet that may not be visible on the screen.

At the very bottom of your screen appears a status line showing **Automatic** (which will be explained later); the default font **Arial**; the default point (or type) size 12; date and time; a row of three buttons that will change the SmartIcons displayed; and **Ready**.

——— 2.3 Columns and rows ———

The letters A, B, C, D, E, F, G, H that appear across the top of the worksheet below the control panel indicate the columns; the numbers 1 to 20 down the left-hand side indicate the rows. The highlighted part of the screen is at location column A row 1, referred to as cell A1.

You can navigate (move) from cell to cell by moving the pointer with the mouse and clicking the left-hand button to highlight the cell, or you can move from cell to cell with the arrow keys on the keyboard.

• Press the **Down Arrow** key twice and the **Right Arrow** key once.

This will move the cell pointer to cell **B3**. The fourth line of the control panel confirms that the highlighted cell is B3 in spreadsheet A (**A:B3**). The cell should be highlighted with a box surrounding it.

• Press your **Home** key to return to cell location **A1**.

Because there are 256 columns (lettered A.....Z, AA, AB...BA, BB and up to IV) and 8192 rows (numbered 1 to 8192), the entire spreadsheet will be too large to fit on to your screen. **Screen dump 2.2** shows the far extremes of the spreadsheet. However, it is easy to move to any part of the spreadsheet without having to press the arrow keys as the next section will show.

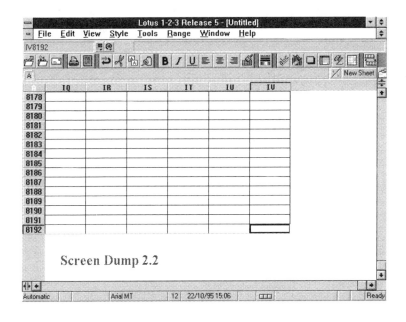

Screen Dump 2.2

The rectangular box that highlights the position of the current cell will be referred to as the **cell pointer**.

– 2.4 Moving around the spreadsheet–

The pointer can be moved around the spreadsheet from cell to cell with cursor control keys as shown. First, you can request a cell location by pressing function key **F5** and then select where you wish to go.

• Press function key **F5**, type T100 and then press the **Enter** key.

As you did this, you will have observed that a **Go To** dialogue box appeared on your screen. Such dialogue boxes are a main feature of Lotus 1-2-3 for Windows.

You will now find yourself looking at a part of the spreadsheet quite distant from A1.

• Press the **Home** key on your keyboard to return to cell A1, often referred to as the Home position.
• Point the mouse arrow at a cell visible on your screen and press the left mouse button. The cell pointer will then highlight the located cell. This is the quickest way of moving around the visible part of the spreadsheet.

You can also move the whole section seen on the screen by using another set of keys:

PgDn or **Page Down**	Move one screen down
PgUp or **Page Up**	Moves one screen up
Tab	Move one screen to the right
Shift & Tab (simultaneously)	Move one screen to the left

• Use the keys listed above to get yourself familiar with navigating around the spreadsheet.
• Press the **Home** key on your keyboard to return to cell A1.

You can also go to the far extremes of the working area of your spreadsheet using your mouse. On the right of the worksheet area you have a scroll box which is a small blank box. Position your mouse pointer on this box and, keeping the mouse key depressed, drag the box down to the end of the bar and let go. You should now be at the end of your spreadsheet. Exactly the same can be done with the bottom bar of your worksheet work area, allowing you to move to the far right of your spreadsheet. Without any data on the spreadsheet at present, it will not be possible to appreciate fully some of the facilities.

- Experiment with the scroll boxes as this will assist you in future work.

The small scroll arrows by these boxes will also allow you to move the spreadsheet around your screen. However, this is better demonstrated when you have some data in your spreadsheet.

Moving the cell pointer off the end of the displayed spreadsheet either vertically or horizontally is known as scrolling. As you scroll, so new columns or row labels will appear and others will disappear. However, you will always be able to get back to them; information out of sight is not lost.

Another key to help you get around your spreadsheet, particularly if you do not have a mouse, is the **End** key. If you press the **End** key followed by the **Down Arrow** key you will go down to the end of the spreadsheet. If you press the **End** key followed by the **Right Arrow** key you will go to the far right of the spreadsheet.

——————— 2.5 Entering text ———————

To begin with you can enter one of four types of data into a cell:

1 **A Number**. This is data of numeric value which can be used in calculations. You will see later in the book that other data, for example, percentage signs, can also be typed in.
2 **A Label**. This is essentially text such as names, addresses and sentences. Such text can contain numbers, or any character that appears on your keyboard. To enter a label, you have to have as the first character one of the following:
   A letter of the alphabet
   ' (apostrophe)
   " (Double quote)
   ^ (Caret – normally appears above the 6)
   \ (Back slash)
   Each of these prefixed characters has a different effect on how the text appears in the cell, which you will discover in due course.
3 **A Formula**. This allows the calculation of figures based on what

else appears in cells in other parts of the spreadsheet. To enter a formula, you will need to have as the first character either + (plus sign) or = (equals) or to enclose the formula between rounded brackets.

4 **A Function**. This is a built-in formula for mathematical, statistical, financial and other work. It begins with an @ sign, and an example of such a function is @SUM(B3..D5), which would sum all numeric values bounded by the area of cells in the range from B3 to D5.

At this point you should be faced with an empty spreadsheet and should position the cell pointer in cell A1. Any entry you type will first be shown in the third line from the top of the screen; the edit bar. Now proceed with the instructions as follows keeping an eye on what is happening on your screen.

• Type MY LOTUS DEMONSTRATION. Note that a large cross and tick appear in the third line, next to the words you have typed. Press the **Enter** key.
• Press the **Down Arrow** key twice, type PRICE and then again press the **Down Arrow** key. Note how this last action entered the text *and* moved down to the next cell.
• Type COST and press the **Down Arrow** key.
• Type PROFIT and press the **Right Arrow** key. At this point the cursor should be in cell B5.

You will notice that what actually appears in the edit bar of the control panel is 'PROFIT not PROFIT. The apostrophe that prefixes the label is an indication that it is a label being entered rather than a number or formula.

Such entries of text into cells are referred to as labels. You will no doubt have noticed that these labels always appear in the far left-hand side of each cell – in other words they are left justified. **Screen dump 2.3** shows what you should see on your screen at this stage.

If your text is not in upper case (capitals), do not worry at this stage, as it will not affect what you do for the rest of the demonstration.

You should be able to see on the screen that the label MY FIRST DEMONSTRATION has been written across adjacent cells. This is permissible only because no entries have been made into these adjacent cells.

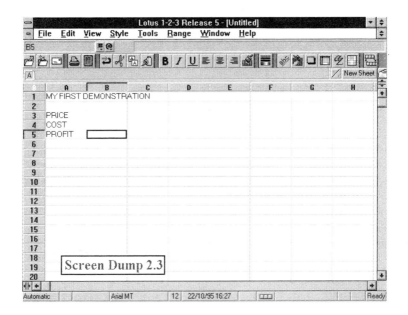

Screen Dump 2.3

2.6 Correcting errors

However careful you are, mistakes are going to be made. There are two basic ways of correcting a cell entry. Suppose that the entry MY FIRST DEMONSTRATION was meant to read MY FIRST LOTUS DEMONSTRATION. To alter it you can select cell A1 by positioning the mouse pointer at cell A1 and clicking your left mouse button and then simply typing the correct label in as though the cell was empty. This will replace the old text with the new entry. Alternatively, you can use a function key to EDIT the cell contents.

● Position the cell pointer at cell A1 and press the function key **F2**.
● Use the **Left Arrow** key to move back along the text until you are positioned at the start of DEMONSTRATION. An alternative way would be to position the mouse arrow in front of DEMONSTRATION and clicking the left button of your mouse (clicking on the space between FIRST and DEMONSTRATION).
● Now type LOTUS and press the **Enter** key.

When the text appears in the control panel in this way, you can use other editing keys such as the **Right Arrow** key, **INSERT** key and the **Back Space** keys.

—————— # 2.7 Entering numbers ——————

Lotus 1-2-3 distinguishes between *values* and *labels* simply by what the first character is. If the first character is a number (0–9) then a value is assumed, but if the first character is alphabetic, then a label is assumed. Hence, if you type: Over 18 years of age, Lotus 1-2-3 assumes this to be a label. However, not all labels beginning with a number will appear in a cell exactly as you wish in this way. To get Lotus 1-2-3 to accept such a string of characters that begins with a numeric character, you will have to include an ' (apostrophe) as the first character. For example, typing in 9.00 - 12.00 would produce -3 (9 minus 12); while '9.00 - 12.00 would be left as 9.00 - 12.00.

- Now enter numbers into each of the cells B3 and B4. To do this, simply place the cell pointer on each cell and type, in turn, the number 69 in cell B3 and 60 in cell B4. On each occasion you must press the **Enter** key, or move the highlighted cell using the arrow keys.

Such numeric entries will be referred to as *values*.

—————— # 2.8 Entering a formula ——————

- Position the cell pointer in cell B5, type +B3-B4 and press the **Enter** key. You have now entered a formula. (Note that this could also have been entered as =B3+B4.)

The calculation of cell B3 minus cell B4 (69 – 60) now appears in cell B5. The edit bar of the control panel shows the formula; the cell shows the result. This demonstrates how the appearance on the spreadsheet alone will not reveal what is actually in the cells.

Lotus 1-2-3 has distinguished your entry in cell B5 as a formula by the fact that it starts with a + or = (or is in brackets) and refers to cell locations. As a technical point, it is worth noting that cell references in formulae are not case sensitive; in other words, (b3-b4) reads exactly the same as (B3-B4).

At this stage you will have a spreadsheet with Labels in cells A1, A3, A4 and A5, values in cells B3 and B4, and a formula in cell B5. On a very small scale this is what spreadsheets are all about. Try altering the price and cost cell, preferably moving from cell to cell with the aid of your mouse to position the cell pointer. Before going any further, experiment by creating more cell entries with extra formulae. For example, add a new cell that shows the profit percentage over selling price +B5/B3*100.

A summary of the special characters to use in formulae would now be useful:

+ Add
– Subtract
* Multiply
/ Divide
(Open bracket (rounded bracket only)
) Close bracket (rounded bracket only)

Building up a formula in Lotus 1-2-3 conforms to all the normal rules of mathematical formulae.

—————— 2.9 Saving your work ——————

In order to save your spreadsheet you will need to select the Save As option from the menu bar at the top of your screen.

• Select the option by positioning the mouse pointer over the menu bar option File and pressing the left mouse button to see the sub-menu 'pulled down' over that part of the screen.

Such menus are called 'pull down menus' because you appear to pull down the menus over the screen.

• As an alternative to using the mouse you can select the menu by holding down the **Alt** key and pressing the character key that is underlined in the menu option required, in this case F. Holding down the **Alt** key and pressing the F key will produce the pull down menu that you produced using your mouse.

Screen dump 2.4 shows the menu that you will see on your screen. The option you want is 'Save As'. This allows you to save your work in a file with a name of your choice. The other options will be explained in later chapters.

• With this menu displayed select Save As either by clicking on the option with your mouse by pressing the **Down Arrow** key or pressing the **A** key (The underlined character in the option Save As).

• Now enter a filename. Give it the name FIRSTGO by typing this in and then pressing the **Enter** key.

If, at a later stage, you wish to save changes you make to the file, you can use the Save option rather than the Save As. This will save the spreadsheet using the same filename.

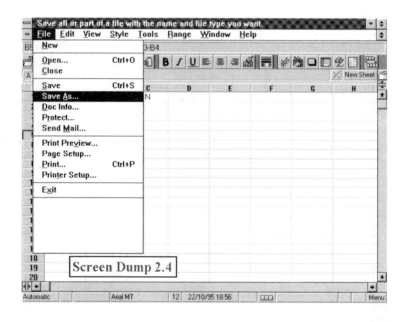

Screen Dump 2.4

When you save your work, Lotus 1-2-3 automatically gives the file an extension name .WK4 unless you specify otherwise. It has also saved the file in a directory for you.

An alternative to using the menu command would be to click on the second SmartIcon from the left.

——— 2.10 Printing your work ———

To complete the process, you can print the spreadsheet. (If you do not have a printer installed then skip this section.)

● Click on the File option from the menu bar. Then select the Print option from the resulting pull-down menu.

● Alternatively, if you prefer not to use the mouse, then select the commands by holding down the **Alt** key and pressing F followed by P for Print.

The various print options will be explained below. For now you will use the shortest and easiest way.

Screen dump 2.5 illustrates the panel that appears. The boxes that need completing require details about pages to be printed and the range to be printed.

Selecting what you want printed is determining what part of the spreadsheet to print. Lotus 1-2-3 defines 'chunks' or blocks of the spreadsheet as ranges. Hence, what you need to do is to define the range to be printed. For this purpose, the mouse will be very useful.

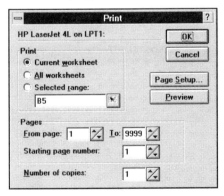

Screen Dump 2.5

Lotus 1-2-3 for Windows will try to 'guess' about what you want printed. At this stage, it assumes you want the spreadsheet printed, as opposed to a range or a collection of worksheets.

The panel that appears on your screen is there to allow you to make any alterations to these settings.

- Click on B5 in the Print box. It will change colour. Now type A1..B5 and then press the **Enter** key.

What this does is to define the range as being the rectangular block of cells that have A1 and B5 at the corners.

- Now click on the **OK** button.

This should activate the printer and a print-out of your work should appear. Meanwhile, on screen you will return to the spreadsheet. If an error has occurred, then it is probably because your printer was not on-line or the computer does not have a printer installed. You can still work with Lotus 1-2-3, but you will not be able to print out your work.

If no error message has appeared and your printer is not printing, then it may be because the output has been stored in a file for later printing from the Print Manager program within Windows. If this is the case, then you will have to activate this program to print. Refer to your Windows manual or *Teach Yourself Windows* for help.

Printing from the spreadsheet can be done more quickly by using the mouse:

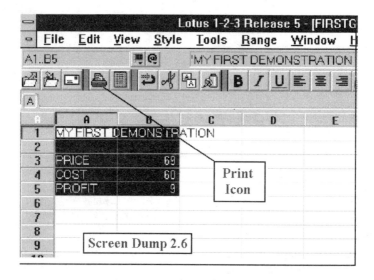

- Return to the spreadsheet by leaving the menu. This should be the state you are at when you have finished printing. If not, press the **Esc** key on your keyboard.
- Click on A1 and, **keeping the left mouse button depressed**, move the pointer to the right and downwards. When you take your finger off the mouse button the area remains in this different colour and has now become **highlighted**. Highlight the block of 10 cells, as in **Screen dump 2.6**.

With the mouse, select the Print icon from the row of SmartIcons. This Print icon is shown as part of **Screen dump 2.6**. This will give you the print dialogue box requiring you to click on **OK** to start printing. The result should be to print the highlighted range.

2.11 Erasing data from a spreadsheet

To produce a more sophisticated spreadsheet, erase the existing data.

- Move the cell pointer to A1 (the Home position).
- Highlight the range, with your mouse, A1 through to B5.
- Select from the menu bar the Edit pull down menu.
- From the pull down menu, select the option Clear. Click on the **OK** button in the Clear dialogue box.

The highlighted range will have cleared. This method of clearing data can be useful if you have made a mistake and wish to re-enter a number of cell entries. Always save the spreadsheet before deleting anything.

There are other ways of deleting ranges of data, such as deleting specified rows or columns, which will be explained at a later stage in the book.

2.12 A new spreadsheet – sales performance

It is now time to try to produce a more sophisticated spreadsheet as shown in **Screen dump 2.7**.

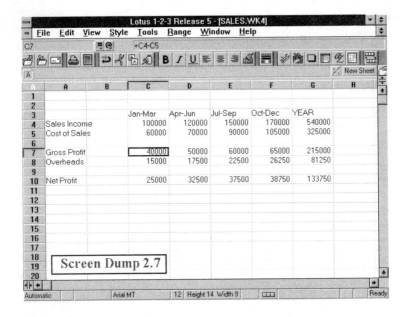

The text and data will have to be typed in as you might do with a word processor. The *calculation* of Gross Profit, Net Profit, and totals are made by Lotus 1-2-3.

- Click on C3 and type the quarterly year heading Jan-Mar. Using the Right Arrow key move to cell D3 and type Apr-Jun. Continue with, Jul-Sep in cell E3, Oct-Dec in cell F3 and YEAR in cell G3.

If you want to enter text into a cell and centre it within that cell rather then leave it left-justified, then you should prefix the text entered with the ^ sign rather than just typing it into the cell. This method of centring text should not be done with the numbers, as Lotus 1-2-3 will not recognise a cell entry prefixed with ^ as a number and so cannot use it for calculations.

- Now type the other labels required: Sales Income in cell A4, Cost of Sales in A5, Gross Profit in cell A7, Overheads in cell A8 and Net Profit in cell A10.

- Now type the data Sales Income and Cost of Sales for each of the four quarters (8 numbers in total).

All the remaining figures will be calculated by Lotus 1-2-3 using formulae that you will type in.

● Click on cell C7 and type +C4-C5. When you press the **Enter** key the correct figure for Gross Profit should appear, i.e. Sales Income less Cost of Sales.

Instead of entering the formulae for the remaining quarters, you will use a different technique.

● Click on G4, type @SUM(C4..F4) and press the **Enter** key. This adds up all the Sales Income figures.
● In cell G5 enter a function for adding the Cost of Sales figures: @SUM(C5..F5).

Now you will use the copying facility to copy the formulae that appears in cell C7 to appear in the cells D7 to G7.

● Click on cell C7, because this is the cell containing the formula you want to copy.
● Select from the menu the option Edit and then from the pull down menu the option Copy.

Although nothing appears to have happened, Lotus 1-2-3 has placed the cell contents into the system **Clipboard**. This is a part of the memory that is used to store data on a temporary basis. What is needed now is to *paste* this into the spreadsheet.

● Highlight the range D7 to G7 using your mouse. To achieve this, click the mouse pointer at cell D7 and, holding the left mouse button down, drag the mouse pointer to cell G7 and then let the mouse button go.
● Now select from the menu bar the option Edit and from the pull-down menu the option Paste.

It should now be apparent that the method and principle of highlighting a range of cells is useful and well worth learning as it can be used to save a considerable amount of keyboard work.

The next stage is to type in a formula for the Overhead figures. For this purpose it has been assumed that Overheads are to be 25% of Cost of Sales. Given this assumption, proceed as follows:

● Click on cell C8 and type the formula +C5*25%. Note how 25% is recorded as 0.25 in the formula in the third line of the control panel. Note also that the correct figure of 15,000 appears in the cell.

Do not use the copy command just yet because there is an even better way of saving time. Net Profit is Gross Profit less Overheads.

- Click on C10, type formula +C7-C8, and press the **Enter** key.

The next stage will be to copy both the Overheads formula and the Net Profit formula for the other three quarters and the year in a single action.

- Highlight the range of cells C8 to C10.
- Now select from the menu bar the option Edit and from the pull-down menu the option Copy.
- Highlight the range of cells D8 to G10. This will define a range of three rows and four columns.
- Select from the menu bar the option Edit and then Paste.

This has enabled you to copy two sets of formulae in a single operation. What you have now done is fundamental to making spreadsheet handling quick and easy to set up. If you are unclear at this stage about what has happened, then give yourself time to experiment.

This now completes the spreadsheet. At this stage you should experiment with the spreadsheet by changing some of the numbers (not the formulae). If you change some of the quarterly Sales Income, or the Cost of Sales figures, the rest of the spreadsheet will adjust by recalculating Gross Profit, Overheads, Net Profits and Year totals.

Now print the spreadsheet as you did in the previous section of this chapter, remembering the sequence of events:

- Highlight what you want printed; click on the Print SmartIcon; click on OK.
- Save your spreadsheet by selecting from the menu bar the option File, then Save As, typing SALES, and clicking OK.

If you have not been able to follow all of this or feel unable to remember how everything was achieved, do not worry. You will get further help and practice as you work through the book.

You will now have performed the typical process involved in producing a spreadsheet, namely:

1 Opening Lotus 1-2-3 for Windows.
2 Preparing a spreadsheet with Labels, Values and Formulae.
3 Entering a varied number of values to see what the results would be.
4 Saving the spreadsheet in a file with a filename.

5 Highlighting the range in the spreadsheet.

6 Printing the highlighted spreadsheet.

2.13 Asking for help

At any time while working through a spreadsheet, Lotus 1-2-3 offers you various levels of help. You can get help by pressing function key **F1**. Doing this produces a screen similar to the one in **Screen dump 2.8**. Release 4 users will see a list of contents rather than a set of icons giving all the help topics.

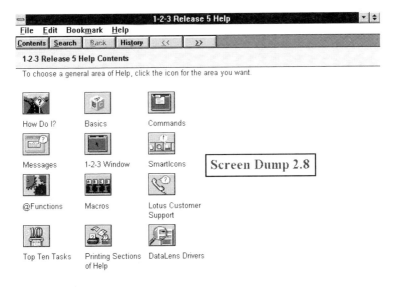

This screen gives you a list of some of the help topics available within Lotus 1-2-3. A small hand will appear as you move the mouse pointer on the screen. When the hand appears over the icon or contents item, you can click to select the help on this topic. While working on many help topics, you will need to use the scroll bar to search through the lists that appear.

You could spend a considerable amount of time looking through the many pages of help available. Pressing the **Esc** key on your keyboard will return you to your spreadsheet at the same position and state you left it.

As mentioned, Lotus 1-2-3 has different levels of help. To see what this means.

- Click on the File option from the menu bar.
- Press function key **F1**.

Now you will get a help screen that tells you what the facilities are in the File pull-down menu.

- Press the **Esc** key to return to the spreadsheet.
- Finally, click on the save SmartIcon to save your most recent changes.
- Now click on the File option from the menu bar, and then select Exit from the pull-down menu. You will quit Lotus 1-2-3 and return to the Windows screen.

In this chapter you created two spreadsheets which have been saved on your disk and can be retrieved at a later stage.

— 2.14 Using Lotus 1-2-3 templates —

This final section can only be worked on if you are using Lotus 1-2-3 Release 5 or later. If you are a Release 4 user, then you should skip this section. Not being able to work on this section will have no harmful impact on the work you do in the remaining chapters.

When you first entered Lotus 1-2-3 from Windows, an opening dialogue box appeared which you were advised to by-pass by clicking on Cancel. This section will give you the opportunity to work with a spreadsheet that has been provided by Lotus 1-2-3 as part of the package. Lotus refers to these spreadsheets as templates, because it gives you a spreadsheet that can be adapted to your own needs.

- Click on the Lotus 1-2-3 icon from Windows so that you enter the spreadsheet.

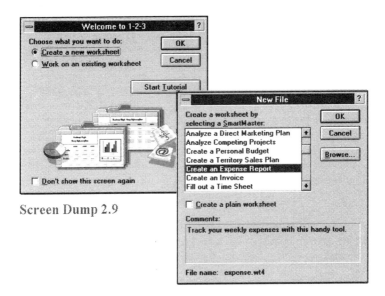

Screen Dump 2.9

The dialogue box that appears is shown in the top part of **Screen dump 2.9**. The opening dialogue box allows you one of three options:

1 **Create a new spreadsheet** from one of the many templates that come with Lotus 1-2-3;

2 **Work on an existing worksheet** that you previously created, such as one of the two you created in this chapter;

3 **Don't show this screen again** so that you go straight into a blank spreadsheet when you enter Lotus 1-2-3 again.

In order to gain an idea of what is possible, you will now inspect a worksheet created for you by Lotus 1-2-3.

● Click on **Create a new spreadsheet** so that a small dot appears to its left and then click on **OK**.

This will create a new dialogue box listing the templates available. To see the whole list, you can either use the **Down Arrow** key on your keyboard or, with your mouse, scroll through the list using the scroll bar to the right of the list of files. As you move through the list, the comments panel will give a brief description of the contents of each worksheet.

- Scroll through the list of files until the file name Create an Expense Report is highlighted, as shown in the lower half of **Screen dump 2.9**.
- Now click on **OK** and wait until the file is loaded and ready for you to inspect it.

The spreadsheet will be copied to another file so that the original is preserved. The new file will then be loaded for you to alter to suit your own requirements. When the file is loaded, a menu will appear. Such a menu is a single sheet of the Lotus 1-2-3 worksheet that has been loaded. Lotus 1-2-3 offers the facility of multiple sheets within a single spreadsheet.

- Click on the button to the left of the Expense Report option.

You will now be moved to another sheet as shown in **Screen dump 2.10** which you can alter at will. The buttons on the spreadsheet can be clicked to perform functions, in the same way as you use icons.

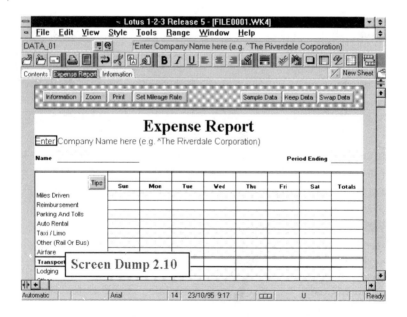

Screen Dump 2.10

- Move through the sheet to give yourself an idea of what can be done. The sheet itself will prompt you about what needs altering, such as the company name. The small **Tips** button can be used to guide you through.

Such spreadsheets give you an idea of what can be achieved and possibly how to go about creating such spreadsheets. At this stage, you will not be able to learn as much from them as you will when you have worked through this book.

- When you have finished working though the worksheet, click on File from the menu bar and then on Exit from the pull down menu.

If you made any alterations to the file, Lotus 1-2-3 will ask you if you want to save the file before you exit. If you click on Yes to this, the file will be saved with your alterations before returning to Windows.

—— 2.15 Chapter summary ——

You have covered the following points:

- How to load Lotus 1-2-3.
- To identify the control panel, menu bar and the SmartIcons at the top of the screen.
- To move around or navigate the spreadsheet in a variety of different ways.
- To highlight cells.
- To distinguish between different types of cell entries: labels, numbers, formulae, and functions.
- To correct typing errors.
- To use the menu bar and pull down menus.
- To define and highlight ranges.
- To use options from the Edit pull-down menu to copy, paste and erase ranges of cells.
- To print spreadsheets.
- To use File commands to Save, Save As and Exit.
- To use SmartIcons to save a file and to print a range.
- To use the Help pages.
- To use Lotus 1-2-3 templates to investigate further what spreadsheets can do.

3

MENUS, PRINTING AND FILING

3.1 Aims of this chapter

One of the principal features of getting to know any package is being able to find your way around a menu system. Lotus 1-2-3 is no exception to this. It has a hierarchical structure of menus which you have already encountered. The first level appears across the menu bar near the top of your screen with the next level pulled down when you implement it. More levels are then produced as you implement further options. This chapter will make you more familiar with the menu structure and help you understand the main options you will commonly need when using the spreadsheet. With many of the menu options, a dialogue box will appear rather than another pull-down menu.

In describing the menu system, emphasis has been placed on saving and retrieving files to and from your hard disk as well as being able to print your spreadsheet. Although these were all introduced in the previous chapter, this chapter investigates the facilities in much more detail.

Although the emphasis in this and future chapters will be on using the menu structure in order to help you get familiar with it, Lotus 1-2-3 also has a large collection of SmartIcons that by-pass the menu system and are designed to help you speed up operations. These will be illustrated alongside the menu system. At the end of this book is a reference section listing all the SmartIcons available and how to get them on to your screen. There will be times while you are working through this chapter that you will need to refer to them.

3.2 Changing the style of your spreadsheet

You have already been introduced to how to write and save a file. Reproduce the spreadsheet depicted in **Screen dump 3.1**. The spreadsheet contains no formulae or functions, just labels and numbers. You will notice that column A is not wide enough to hold the label Wednesday; leave it as it stands for now because you will learn how to widen the cell.

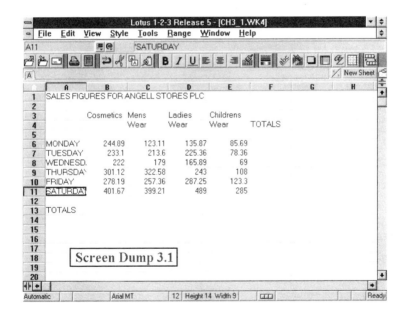

Screen Dump 3.1

Before saving the file, you will use the menu structure to set all numbers in the spreadsheet to two decimal places and widen column A.

The first step before saving will be to Format all numbers to two decimal places. This involves altering the Style of the spreadsheet.

- Highlight the range of cells where the numbers are stored: B6 to E11. At this stage it is worth discovering that this can be done via your keyboard. Holding down the **Shift** key, press the **Arrow** keys to move the cell pointer and highlight the block.
- Click on the Style option from the menu bar. Then Number Format.
- In the dialogue box, click on **Fixed** in the **Format** box.

The **Format** box contains a list of available formats and the Fixed option is in the list. The scroll bar to the right of the **Format** box allows you to scroll up and down this list with your mouse. When you have found the format wanted, the mouse is again used to highlight it, in this case Fixed, by pointing the mouse pointer over it and clicking the left mouse button.

At this stage you should have something similar to **Screen dump 3.2** which shows the **Number Format** dialogue box.

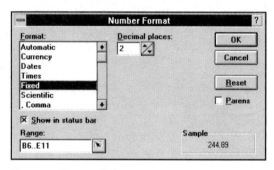

Screen Dump 3.2

The rest of the settings are correct: the default of 2 decimal places and the range B6..E11.

What this shows is that you have selected a Fixed Format that will fix a range of numbers to two decimal places.

- Click on the **OK** button, or press the **Enter** key.

All the numbers will have been expanded to two decimal places. Next, you can widen column A so that the whole of the word Wednesday can be seen. Lotus 1-2-3 starts off with all columns set to 9 characters wide. You will need to have column A at least 10 characters wide.

- Click on cell C8.
- Click on Style in the menu bar, then Column Width.
- Click on the dot next to Fit widest entry and then click on the **OK** button. The column will expand to accommodate the word Wednesday.

Formatting numbers and sizing columns to fit the widest entries can be performed using SmartIcons, and these will be explained later.

—————— ## 3.3 The menu structure ——————

This method of altering the appearance of the spreadsheet will be discussed again on many occasions and, in particular, later in this chapter. You should by now be getting a good appreciation of how the menu structure and the dialogue boxes work. In most cases, you will pull down a menu, select an option and then complete a dialogue box of settings (or parameters). Or you will simply click on a SmartIcon that you can position above, below, or on either side of the working area.

Remember when you use the menu bar you will notice that one character in each option is underlined. If you hold down the **Alt** key and then press the letter underlined, this will implement the pull-down menu.

When dialogue boxes appear, their options will also have a single character underlined. You can use your keyboard to select these by holding down the **Alt** key and then pressing the appropriate letter.

While working with the menus there will be an important source of help available to you. You will see prompts given in the control panel at the top of your screen. These prompts will give you basic instructions as to what input is expected and is often enough to remind you about the detailed operation of many facilities. Release 5 users also have the benefit of small balloons appearing when the mouse is positioned over a SmartIcon, giving information on its function.

Function key **F1** gives you help at any stage and is, in itself, a menu structure of help facilities. It is time well spent exploring the help structure as it is a means that will often solve some awkward problems.

————— 3.4 Saving a file —————

This next section explains in a little more detail the process of saving your file.

● Click on the File option from the menu bar. Then select the Save As option, and type the name STORE.

You will notice that there are many options available in the File pull-down menu. A little explanation is now in order.

New. This opens a new spreadsheet. When a new spreadsheet is started, an old one remains. You will experiment with this in a later chapter.

Open. This allows you to open a spreadsheet that already exists without losing the one you are currently working with.

Close. This closes the current spreadsheet file. This option will prompt you for a filename if you have not saved the most current version.

Save. This will allow you to save a file that you have either saved before or one that you have retrieved. In other words, it saves the file under the same name previously given. If the spreadsheet has no name (i.e. is Untitled), you will be asked for a filename.

Save As. This will save a spreadsheet with another file name or will save a spreadsheet that has not previously been saved. You will always be prompted for a filename using this option.

Doc Info. This is only available with Release 5 and is used to add documented information to your file. If you select this option prior to saving your file, then a dialogue box appears as shown in **Screen dump 3.3**.

The information on the grey background is generated by Lotus 1-2-3 and is largely self-evident. The panels require input from you. In the illustration shown in screen dump 3.3 the panels have been used to record basic details about the spreadsheet set up in this chapter. When the file is saved, this documentation becomes a permanent feature of the spreadsheet and can be seen by selecting Doc Info again from the File pull-down menu.

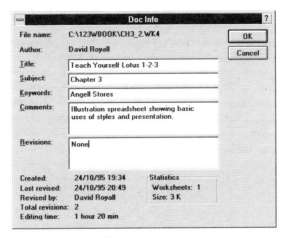

Screen Dump 3.3

The other options require a little more investigation before you can make full use of them. However, knowing what they can do will increase your understanding of basic concepts. [Some of the remaining options may differ according to the version of the package you have.]

Protect. This allows you to protect a file from being altered in certain ways. If you have spent time creating a spreadsheet that you want to use for reference later, then protecting it from unwanted alterations and deletion can be a useful safeguard. You can remove the protection at a later stage.

Send Mail. This allows you to send a spreadsheet, or parts of it, to other users and other applications. The use of this requires extra software in addition to the Lotus 1-2-3 spreadsheet. Consequently this facility is not a topic for this book.

Print Preview. This allows you to see your file as it will appear when it is printed.

Page Setup. This lets you determine how the spreadsheet will appear when printed. Lotus 1-2-3 will set the page layout for you, but this allows you to alter things like headers and footers, orientation and margins.

Print. This prints your spreadsheet or a range of the spreadsheet that has been defined. It can also be used to print your graphs.

Printer setup. This is used to set up your printer differently from the way it is set up by the Windows printer control.

Exit. Returns to the Windows screen.

At the foot of this menu may appear a list of files. This allows you to quickly open a file. The list is generated from the most recent files you have used. As you work more with Lotus 1-2-3, you will see this list grow and change.

You will not need most of these options, but they are there to allow you to tailor the spreadsheet package more effectively to your particular needs.

• Having saved STORE.WK4, click on Close from the File pull-down menu.

At this point you should have an empty spreadsheet.

Opening a file is the reverse of saving one.

• Click on File and then select Open.

You will see the Open File dialogue box. If your file does not appear in the Filename box, it may be because there is not enough room in the window to display all the available file names. Use the arrow keys to scroll through the menu names. As an alternative to the arrow keys, you can use your mouse to move the box between the up and down arrows.

• Select the file saved as STORE by clicking on it with your mouse to highlight the file name. Then click on the **OK** button.

The STORE.WK4 file should now reappear on your screen.

— 3.5 Expanding your spreadsheet —

Now you can add to the spreadsheet. First, type in formulae for the totals in column F.

• Click on cell F6.

• Type the start of the function: @SUM(.

Instead of typing in the range where the numbers are located, you can highlight the range in the same way as you have highlighted ranges before.

• Use either your arrow keys or mouse to position the cell pointer on cell B6.
• Now hold down the left mouse button and move the mouse pointer to E6 so that the range is highlighted. (Holding down the **Shift** key and pressing the **Arrow** keys can be used as an alternative to your mouse.)
• Let go of your mouse button and press the **Enter** key. (Or let go of the **Shift** and **Arrow** keys if you are using your keyboard.)

The desired result should be to add the numbers in the column. Check that this is so. The function in cell F6 should be @SUM(B6..F6).

The next objective is to copy this formula to the range F7..F11.

• Position the cell pointer at cell F6 where the formula has been entered. This is the one you need to copy.
• Click on Edit from the menu bar and then select Copy.

This has stored the formula in the Clipboard and would appear to have done nothing.

• Highlight the range of cells F7 to F11.
• Click on Edit from the menu bar and then select Paste.

You now have daily totals for the complete store. Next you should type in formulae to add up the weekly totals for each department, and one for the overall sales of the store.

• Click on cell B13 and enter a formula. Then click on the Formulae SmartIcon, then click on Sum from the pull-down menu, as shown in **Screen dump 3.4**.
• Highlight cells B6 to B11 and then click on the Tick icon. The row total should now appear in cell B13 and the formula @SUM(B6..B11) in the control panel. Copy the formula in cell B13 to the range C13 to F13.
• Type a label, right justified, in cell A13 as TOTALS. Remember, to right justify you need to prefix the label with ".

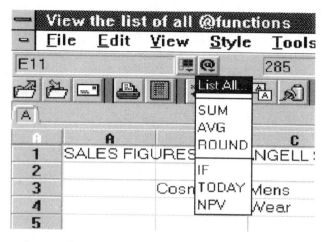

Screen Dump 3.4

You will also notice at this stage that the format of the numbers determined by the formulae is not to two places of decimal. Moreover, the figures are not quoted in £ sterling, the next stage will be to format all numbers to two places of decimal as currency.

• Highlight the range of cells from B6 to F13.
• Click on the Style option from the menu bar.
• Select the Number Format option from the pull-down menu.

Screen dump 3.5 shows a dialogue box completed for the number format required in this instance. Release 4 users will not have the choice of Currency on this dialogue box.

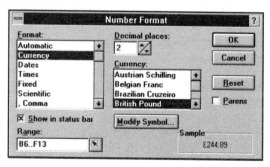

Screen Dump 3.5

- Click on Currency in the Format box. You will see that the Decimal places box is already 2.
- If you are a Release 5 user, then select the Currency as British Pound. You may have to scroll through the list to find this currency.

The remaining settings in the dialogue box are as you need them, hence you can leave them as they are.

- Click on the **OK** button to activate the format and return to the spreadsheet.

Next, you will remove the Grid lines that appear on the spreadsheet.

- Click on the View option from the menu bar. Then select the Set View Preferences option.

The resulting dialogue box allows you to make considerable changes to the appearance of your spreadsheet.

- To remove the grid lines, click on the Grid Lines box. When there is no cross in the box, the grid lines will not appear on the spreadsheet.

The spreadsheet should now look similar to that shown in **Screen dump 3.6**.

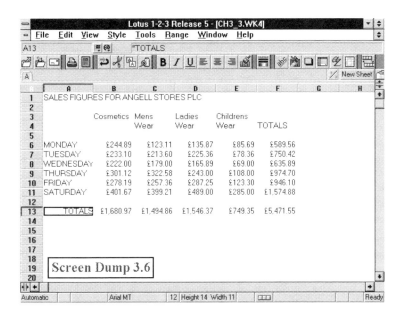

Before moving on to the next section, it is now a useful exercise to take a quick peak at what you had before making these additions.

The first stage will be to save your file under a different name:

- Click on the File option from the menu bar. Then select the Save As option.
- Save the file with the file name STORE2.
- Click on the file. Then select Open. From the list of files, select STORE again, and click the OK button to open the file.

You now have two copies of the same file. The last one you opened will be visible on your screen. This is the one you started with.

- Click on the Window option from the menu bar. [If there is a Pick option showing, then select it. Newer versions of Lotus 1-2-3 do not require this.]

This now presents you with the files open for you to pick from. If you pick STORE2 then you will be returned to that sheet. (In an application of this kind, the store could, for instance, keep a spreadsheet for each week of the year. You could then open different weeks and make various comparisons.)

You can hop back and forth between spreadsheets making alterations to one without affecting the others. You can also work in either spreadsheet without effecting the other. Chapter 9 has a section on how you can link formulae between two spreadsheets.

3.6 Relative and absolute cell addresses

At the moment, keep both spreadsheets open and make sure that you have selected the most recently created spreadsheet to work with: namely, STORE2. This section will examine the more advanced features of copying formulae from one part of the spreadsheet to another.

On row 15 you will create a new formula that expresses each department total as a percentage of the grand total. The departmental percentage is the departmental total divided by the overall total and expressed as a percentage. In this exercise, you will need to enter a formula in cell B15 to express this formula and then copy the formula across the other departments. The problem with this is that when you copy the formula the relative position of the overall total will alter for each department.

In a formula, a reference to a cell that does not change when you copy the formula is called an *Absolute* reference. An absolute reference always refers to the same cell or range. To create an absolute cell reference, type a $ (dollar sign) before the column letter and row number when you write the formula. Here, F13 becomes the absolute cell reference in the formula needed in cell B13.

• Highlight cell B15 and type in the formula +B13/$F$13.

The result will appear as a decimal and will need to be formatted as a percentage. This will be done later.

• Now copy cell B15 to the range C15 to E15.

As an exercise, repeat the two steps just undertaken but with the formula +B13/F13 in cell B15. Try to see what has happened by looking at each formula through the range. Then go back to correct the formula.

Now you need to alter the format so that percentages are shown.

• Highlight the range of cells as B15 to E15.
• Click on the Style option from the menu bar. Then select Number Format.
• Click on the Percent option.
• Set the number of Decimal places to be 0 (zero). Click on the **OK** button.

As a next task, you will introduce two new departments, Electrical and Furniture. These two new departments will appear between Cosmetics and Men's Wear. To do so, you will need to insert two new columns.

• Click on Column letter C. The entire column is now highlighted.
• Click on the Edit option from the menu bar. Then select Insert.
• Repeat this to insert a second column.

The effect of this has been to insert two columns and shift the columns to the right two columns along. You will also note that the formulae in all cells have been preserved.

• Now type in the new headings for Electrical and Furniture departments. Try the following, as these numbers will prove useful in the remaining parts of this chapter:

	Electrical	Furniture
Monday	322	0
Tuesday	291	1,200
Wednesday	228.23	100
Thursday	256.12	499.99
Friday	331.2	5,400
Saturday	410.1	12,099

If the new numbers entered do not have the format in the same way as the others you will need to format the new range for currency.

Now the end column is off the screen because the spreadsheet is too wide. As a further demonstration of the windows facilities, you will next create a vertical window in column B that allows you to move around the table of figures and be able to see the days of the week remain in the left-most part of the screen.

- Click on column letter B. The entire column is highlighted.
- Click on the View option from the menu bar, then click on Split. Click on Vertical in the Type box of the dialogue box. Then click on the **OK** button.

You have now split your screen into two windows with both windows showing the same spreadsheet, but at differing points. To move between windows you can either press function key **F6** or click on the window you want to work in and press the mouse button. The advantage of having the two versions of the same spreadsheet open is that you can keep the days of the week visible in the left-hand window, while you scroll the right-hand window from side to side so that you can work on all the figures and still see what day of the week they relate to.

To finish the job off, you need to complete the departmental totals and percentages for the two new departments. This time use the SmartIcons on the control panel.

- Make sure you are in the right-hand window.
- Highlight cells B13 to B15. Now copy this by clicking on the Copy SmartIcon. Highlight cells C13 to E13 and click on the Paste SmartIcon. Use **Screen dump 3.7** to identify where the Copy and Paste SmartIcons are located.

Notice how not only the formula has been copied, but also the formats (currency, decimal points, etc.) defined for the cells you have copied from.

At this stage you should have a spreadsheet similar to that shown in **Screen dump 3.7**.

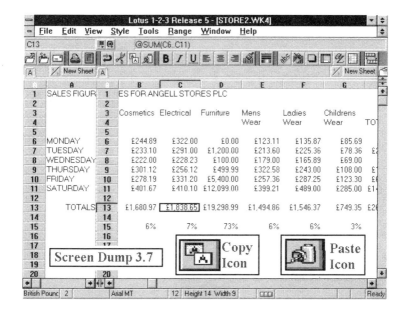

3.7 Using windows to see two spreadsheets

Before proceeding any further, it is wise to save your latest efforts again so that nothing is lost.

● Click on the Save SmartIcon.

At this stage you will have saved the current version as STORE2 again. Remember that STORE, which was the earlier version, will also be on disk and is still open.

● Click on the <u>W</u>indow option from the menu bar. Then select <u>T</u>ile.

The result should be similar to that shown in **Screen dump 3.8**.

You can hop freely between these two spreadsheets by clicking on them the same way as you hopped between the windows in the same spreadsheet.

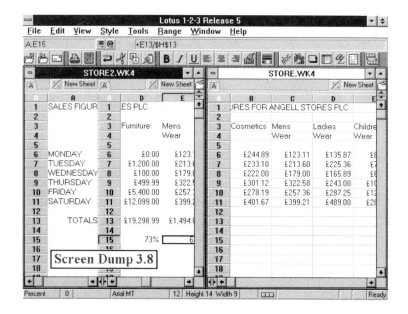

Screen Dump 3.8

From the <u>W</u>indows option you can also select <u>C</u>ascade to see the spreadsheets one behind the other. In Chapter 9 you will see how Lotus 1-2-3 allows you to set up something similar to this by giving a spreadsheet a three-dimensional effect of multiple sheets within a single spreadsheet.

- Return to the tiled windows. Ensure that you are in the old spreadsheet - STORE.WK4.

- Close the file. The quickest way to do this is to double click (i.e. press the left mouse button twice) on the minus sign in the line containing the file title, in this case STORE.WK4.

This will leave your screen half empty. To fill the screen with your spreadsheet:

Either

- Move the mouse pointer gently to the edge of the spreadsheet until you see a double headed arrow on it. Then, holding the mouse button down, drag the mouse to the right to fill your screen with the spreadsheet, rather like pulling a curtain across a rail.

Or

- Click on the maximise button in the right-hand corner of the line containing the file title.

3.8 Fonts, presentation and printing

The final section of this chapter will investigate the way you can alter the look of your spreadsheet. What you are able to achieve here may be a little restricted depending on the capabilities of your computer and printer.

To see more clearly what is going on, close the vertical window to have the whole spreadsheet showing on the screen.

- Click on View from the menu bar. Then select Clear Split.

In order to see the whole spreadsheet on your screen you will need to alter the width of some of your columns.

Lotus 1-2-3 allows you to alter the column widths with your mouse in a similar way to the method of opening your spreadsheet across to fill the screen.

- Click on column letter A. The entire column is now highlighted. Move the mouse pointer carefully to the right edge of the box showing column letter A. The pointer turns into a black pointer.
- Holding the left mouse button down, drag the column heading to the right to widen the cell. When you let go of the mouse button, the new width will set accordingly.
- Go through each of the other columns reducing the widths where you can.

Next you will have the opportunity to play around with the visual impact of what you have on the screen. This will vary in accordance with your system, so you will be left to experiment for yourself after a few preliminary instructions.

Look at **Screen dump 3.9** to get the idea of what can be achieved. Do not concern yourself if you are unable to achieve this; your system may be different from the one that was used for the purpose of illustrating this book.

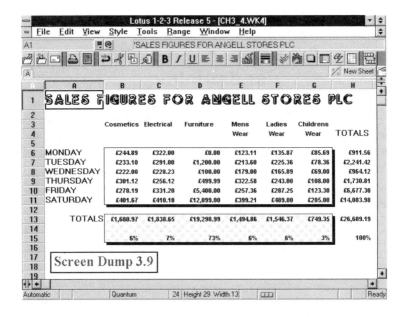

Screen Dump 3.9

Most of the actions taken to achieve the above have been done with the Style options from the menu bar. These are:

    Fonts & Attributes
    Lines & Color
    Gallery
    Alignment

First, you should discover the available fonts. This determines style and size of letters and numbers. There are numerous fonts.

To change the font:

• Highlight the range of cells where you want the text to have a different font. For example, click on A1 then click on Style from the menu bar. Then click on Font & attributes.

The selection of fonts will be listed on your screen. The default font is Arial. Scroll through the list of Faces to get an idea of the number of fonts available. The sample box will show you how the font looks. The default size is 12 point, so the 24-point font will be twice the size, while the 10 point size is proportionately smaller.

• Click on a larger Size (24 point, for example).
• Click on a Face type (Quantum, for example).
• Make any other alterations you wish and then click on the **OK** button.

The effect should be instant.

Now change the alignment so as to centre the text where the columns headings are:

• Highlight cells B3 to H4.
• Click on Style. Then click on Alignment.
• Select Center in the Horizontal box in the Alignment dialogue box, and click on the **OK** button.

For boxed and shaded figures:

• Highlight cells B6 to G11.
• Click on Style. Then select Lines & Color.
• You can select a different style for any of the lines by clicking on the appropriate boxes in the dialogue box. Pick a thin, thick or double line. Change the colour. Add shading.

The Gallery option in the Style menu contains pre-formatted styles that you can apply to any spreadsheet. These are well worth experimenting with.

• Finally, print your spreadsheet.

Before printing the spreadsheet, you will have a go at altering the way the spreadsheet appears on the paper and enhance the information that is printed. This requires you to enter the Page Setup part of Lotus 1-2-3.

● Click on the File option from the menu bar. Then click on Page Setup.

This now presents you with a dialogue box as shown in **Screen dump 3.10**, which has been altered to affect the way the spreadsheet is printed.

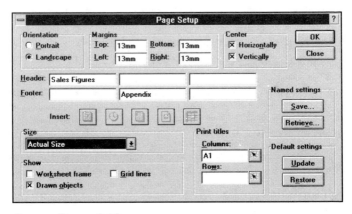

Screen Dump 3.10

Starting at the top right of the dialogue box, the **Orientation** has been set as Landscape, rather than Portrait: printing sideways across the paper rather than from top to bottom. The margins that appear are the default margins which can be altered. The Centre settings of Horizontally and Vertically means that Lotus 1-2-3 will centre the output on the paper centrally down the paper (vertically) and centrally along the paper (horizontally); leaving them both off will cause output to appear as near to the top left of the paper as the margins will allow.

The Header allows a heading to appear at the top of the paper. The heading Sales Figures in **Screen dump 3.10** indicates this is to appear at the top left of each page. If you want a header to appear in the centre, then the text should be entered in the centre box; or if you want it on the right, the right-hand box. The Footer works in exactly the same way as the header, but the text is printed at the bottom of each page.

The Save button to the right and below Named Settings of the dialogue box allows you to save all the entered parameters so that you are able to call them back at a later time using Retrieve. Alternatively, if you click on the Update button below default setting update, the settings in the dialogue box become the new defaults, which can be reversed using the Restore option.

Columns and Rows can be printed as part of the output title by entering the Columns and Rows in the Print Titles Boxes. For example, if the title is on Row 1, then enter 1 or A1 in the Rows box.

The paper Size can be selected from a choice and will be restricted to the kind of printer you have attached to your system. Also, you can have the choice of including as part of your output the worksheet frame (the column and row headings), the Grid Lines and Drawn objects (graphic images).

- Make any necessary changes to the layout and then click on **OK**.

You should now be back at your spreadsheet.

- Highlight the range where the data appears.
- Click on the Print SmartIcon.
- Check that the dialogue box has the range set to print the whole spreadsheet and, if any settings are wrong, alter them by entering the range to print to include the whole spreadsheet.
- Click on the **OK** button to start printing.

As an alternative to printing, you can always preview the spreadsheet on your screen.

- Click on the Print Preview SmartIcon. Then click on the **OK** button.

This will show you what the printed output should look like. Such a facility saves a lot of time as you do not have to wait for the printer to see if any effects you have chosen really are what you want. It also saves wasting paper.

Screen dump 3.11 shows the printed output produced in Landscape rather than Portrait. In other words, the printed output would appear sideways down the paper. This is useful when the output is too wide for portrait mode.

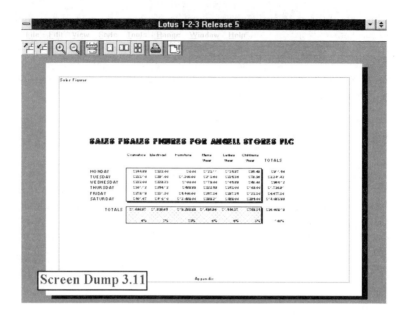

At the top of the preview screen are a number of SmartIcons. The two left ones allow you to move from page to page. As you only have a single page, this is of no apparent use here. The two magnifying glasses allow you to zoom in and out on the sheet. The next one is the Page Setup icon; the printer icon to print the page; while the rightmost icon returns you to your spreadsheet.

● Click on the Print icon and print the page.

Lotus 1-2-3's ability to give such a good visual presentation will be further developed in the next chapter when you go on to explore graphics. For now, spend some more time experimenting with what you have before you.

3.9 Chapter summary

This chapter has concentrated on how Lotus 1-2-3 commands are organised in a hierarchical menu structure with dialogue boxes for you to alter at will. Finding your way around menus will become easier through practice and experience.

In both file handling and printing, you will have examined only a part of what can be achieved. However, in both cases you have seen the important principles involved.

In this chapter you have:

- understood the menu bar, pull-down menus, and dialogue boxes.
- widened columns.
- used Save and Retrieve to handle files in different ways.
- used Copy and Paste to copy both relative and absolute formulae,
- used Format to allow for currency and changed or set the currency symbol.
- used commands to insert columns.
- split the screen to help you with extra large spreadsheets.
- used windows to inspect more than one spreadsheet at a time in Tile and Cascade.
- altered the physical appearance of a spreadsheet with different fonts, lines, colours and shading.
- printed and previewed a spreadsheet in landscape and portrait.

4

STATISTICS AND GRAPHS

Lotus 1-2-3 has an extremely useful graphing facility for putting fine touches to your data. The purpose of this chapter is to familiarise you with these facilities and develop your spreadsheet skills further.

Apart from being able to draw graphs, you will see that once the graph has been set up, it is instantly redrawn as the data change. In Chapter 8 you will return to graphs and take the whole process a stage further.

A good deal of this chapter will require you to highlight ranges of cells with your mouse in order to make efficient use of the facilities contained via the pull-down menus or with the SmartIcons.

——— 4.2 Reading the indicator ———

On the bottom line of the screen – the status bar – in the right-hand corner appears the word 'Ready'. This mode indicator changes as you perform different functions. Here are the most common indications:

Indicator	Mode
EDIT	You pressed **F2** (EDIT) to edit an entry; you are entering or editing text in a text box; or you made an incorrect entry.
ERROR	Lotus 1-2-3 is displaying a message. Choose Help or press **F1** (HELP) to get help; select OK to clear the message.

LABEL   You are entering a label.

MENU   You clicked the menu bar; or pressed **Alt** or **F10** (MENU); or in a dialogue box, you are selecting an element from a list box or check box, option button, or command button.

POINT   You are specifying a range before choosing a command, while working in a dialogue box, or while entering a formula.

READY   Lotus 1-2-3 is ready for you to enter data or choose a command.

VALUE   You are entering a value.

WAIT   Lotus 1-2-3 is completing a command or process, such as saving a file.

Refer to the mode indicator if you get stuck.

4.3 Entering the statistics

• Open a new spreadsheet by clicking on <u>F</u>ile, then select <u>N</u>ew. Look at **screen dump 4.1** to see what you will be aiming at in terms of the data for the first exercise.

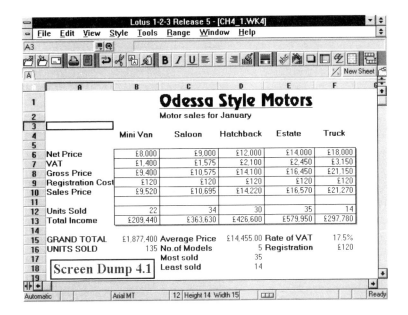

Screen Dump 4.1

The spreadsheet shows the sales figures for a business selling five ranges of motor vehicles. The data on the spreadsheet will be used to give graphical presentation of the Sales Income this business has secured over the January period.

Before moving on, think about how the data is to be set out and, in particular, which data areas are to be calculated by Lotus 1-2-3 and which are to be typed in by you.

- If your spreadsheet working area is not maximised already, click on the maximise button so that the spreadsheet area gives you more area to work with.
- Click on cell C1, type Odessa Style Motors, and press the **Enter** key.
- Click on Style from the main menu bar, then select Fonts & Attributes.
- From the Fonts & Attributes dialogue box, select the following (use **Screen dump 4.2** as a guide):
- Click on Face and, from the list of fonts, select Renfrew. Set the Size as 24 and click on Underline.
- Click on the **OK** button.
- Click on cell C2 and type Motor sales for January.

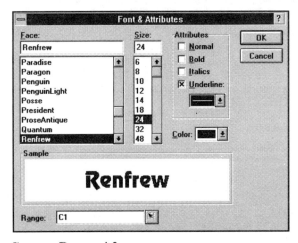

Screen Dump 4.2

When entering the text into cells, the use of the backspace key allows you to delete characters while entering the text. Also, if the text is already on the spreadsheet and you want it altered, you can use the editing facilities of function key **F2** or your mouse to put it right. Altering text in cells will not alter the font settings you made earlier.

- Click on the SmartIcons to change the label in cell C2 to bold or italic.
- Commence with the following entries:

In cell	Type	Press
B4	Mini Van	Right Arrow
C4	Saloon	Right Arrow
D4	Hatchback	Right Arrow
E4	Estate	Right Arrow
F4	Truck	ENTER

- Highlight cells B4 to F4.
- Click on the Bold SmartIcon to change them to bold and then click on the Centre Text SmartIcon to centre the text in each of the cells.

Click on cell A6 and proceed with the following entries:

In cell	Type in	Then press
A6	Net Price	Down Arrow
A7	VAT	Down Arrow
A8	Gross Price	Down Arrow
A9	Registration Cost	Down Arrow
A10	Sale Price	Down Arrow twice
A12	Units sold	Down Arrow
A13	Total Income	Down Arrow twice
A15	GRAND TOTAL	Down Arrow
A16	UNITS SOLD	Right Arrow twice, Up Arrow
C15	Average Price	Down Arrow
C16	No. of Models	Down Arrow
C17	Most sold	Down Arrow
C18	Least Sold	

Click on

| E15 | Rate of VAT | Down Arrow |

- Mark all text in bold by highlighting the ranges and clicking on the Bold SmartIcon.

VAT is, of course, an acronym for Value Added Tax and is a percentage sales tax. In other words, a VAT rate of 10 will mean 10% is to be added to the price. Such rates alter from time to time, so it will be important to allow for these changes in spreadsheets that use them.

Having typed all this in, it should be apparent that Column A is too tight and needs widening.

- Highlight the range A4 to E18.
- Click on Style, then Column Width. In the dialogue box Click on Fit Widest entry, than click on **OK**.

Next you must type in numbers and formulae.

— 4.4 Good spreadsheet practice —

Cell F15 will be used to store the current rate of VAT.

- Click on cell F15 and type in the percentage rate as 17.5%. Include the percentage sign.

Older versions Lotus 1-2-3 will convert this percentage to a fraction by dividing it by 100, thus the number 0.175 will appear in the cell. If this happens, you will need to format this cell to appear on the spreadsheet as a percentage:

- Click on cell F15.
- Click on Style, then Number Format. Select Percent in the Format box, 1 in the Decimal places box, then click on the **OK** button.

You will use this cell later to calculate the VAT to be charged on each car. This is good practice when designing a spreadsheet and it will be discussed further shortly.

The figures you are about to type in are to be displayed in currency format, so you will need to format the range of cells where these are to appear in currency format and to two decimal places. Lotus 1-2-3 allows you to do this format before you enter the numbers.

- Highlight cells B6 to F10.
- Click on Style, the Number Format, then Currency in the Format box, then set the Decimal places to 0 and click on **OK**.
- Type in the basic prices of the vehicles as whole numbers in cells B6 to F6.

If the columns are too narrow, a row of ********* will warn you. When this appears, widen the appropriate column to reveal the numbers.

Now it is time to calculate the amount of VAT payable on the Net Price of each vehicle. Cell F15 is an absolute cell for all vehicles. The VAT payable will be the price in the appropriate relative cell multiplied by the figure in absolute cell F15. If the rate of VAT were to alter, you can simply type the new rate in cell F15 (not forgetting to include the % sign) and the VAT amounts will automatically be recalculated in row 7. This is what is meant by adapting good spreadsheet practice.

- Click on cell B7, type in the formula +B6*$F$15, and click on the tick icon.

Because the VAT cell is absolute, you can copy the formula to the rest of the vehicles and the VAT element will remain constant.

- With cell B7 highlighted, click on the Copy SmartIcon.
- Highlight cells B7 to F7, then click on the Paste SmartIcon.

Examine each of the formulae in the range of cells B7 to F7 to appreciate how the concept of relative and absolute cell locations work. Also, try altering the rate of VAT, to appreciate what is happening.

- Click on cell B8 and type in the formula +B6+B7. This will add the VAT to the basic price.
- Now Copy the formula in cell B8 to the range C8 to F8.

Row 9 will contain the registration cost which will be the same for all vehicles. It would again be good practice to use a single cell to reference this cost.

- Click on cell E16, type in the label Registration and click on the tick icon.
- Change this text to bold to match the rest of the labels.
- Click on cell F16, type in the number 120 into cell F16.
- Make this cell a currency format to 0 decimal places.
- Click on cell B9 and type in the formula +$F$16.
- Now Copy the formula in cell B9 to the range C9 to F9.

The formulae in the range of cells B9 to F9 contain only one single cell reference which has been fixed as absolute. You could just as easily have placed the number 120 into each cell. However, if the registration cost were to change, you would have six values to alter. Using this technique, you will have only one cell value to alter.

You can now arrive at the sale price.

- Click on cell B10 and enter the formula +B8+B9 to add the Registration cost to the Gross Price.
- Copy the formula in cell B10 to the range C10 to F10.
- Click on cell B13 and type in the formula +B10*B12, then click on the tick icon. This multiplies the Sale Price by Units Sold to give Total Income.
- Now Copy the formula in cell B13 to the range C13 to F13.
- Finally, format the cells B13 to F13 as currency to zero decimal places.

In **Screen dump 4.1** the range of numbers from B6 to F13 have been boxed with a drop shadow and the grid lines have been removed. To do this

- Highlight cells B6 to F13.

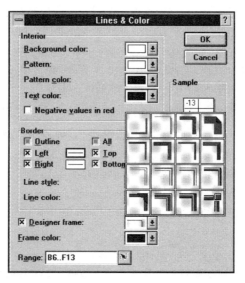

Screen Dump 4.3

- Click on Style, then Lines & Color.

Screen dump 4.3 shows the dialogue box that sets up the drop shadow border and lines around the cells.

- In the Border box in the Lines & Color dialogue box, click on All from the Border panel. This will create a line around all the cells in the highlighted range.
- Now click on Designer frame to reveal 16 frames you can select from. Click on the one on the top row, the second from the left, to get the drop shadow.
- Now click on the **OK** button.

To remove all the grid lines from the spreadsheet:

- Click on View, then Set View Preferences.
- To remove the grid lines, click on Grid Lines in the Show in Current file of the Set View Preferences dialogue box. Use **Screen dump 4.4** as a guide to this.

Altering the Show in Current file parameters will alter the screen appearance for this spreadsheet only; unless you click on the Make default button to set it as default for all future sessions. Alternatively, the Show in 1-2-3 parameters will automatically alter the appearance in all future sessions until altered again.

The top part of your spreadsheet should now be complete. Save it. The next stages, before producing your first graph, will be to introduce you to a few new functions that you may well find useful in future.

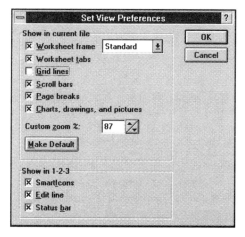

Screen Dump 4.4

——— 4.5 Some new functions ———

Cells B15 and B16 will contain the total income and units sold, respectively. These will be calculated using the function SUM, which you have used before.

- Click on cell B15.
- Click on the @ SmartIcon, then SUM.
- Highlight the cells B13 to F13, then click on the tick SmartIcon.
- Click on Style, then Number Format, then Currency, then 0 Decimal places, then click on the **OK** button. If the column is not wide enough, click on column letter B to highlight the whole column and widen the column.
- Repeat this for the units sold in cell B16. The cell has to sum up the range B12 to F12.

In cell D15 a function can be typed in that will calculate the average selling price based on the figures in the cells B10 to F10. Lotus 1-2-3 will add up the five prices and divide by five. The function that will do this automatically is AVG.

- Click on cell D15.
- Click on the @ SmartIcon, then AVG.
- Highlight cells B10 to F10, then click on the tick icon.
- Format this cell as currency, as before, this time to 2 decimal places.

Check with a calculator that this is correct.

Lotus 1-2-3 can add up the number of cell entries in a range using the COUNT function. In cell D16 you want to total number of models in the range B4 to F4. Although obvious at this stage, there may be an instance when you want to count entries in a much bigger range where some of the cells have no entries.

- Click on cell D16.
- Click on the @ SmartIcon, then on List All.
- In the @ Function box, scroll until you see COUNT. Click on COUNT and then click on the **OK** button.
- Highlight cells B4 to F4, then click on the tick icon.

Finally, in cells D17 to D18 you want the maximum and minimum numbers, respectively, in the range B12 to F12.

- Click on cell D17.
- Click on the @ SmartIcon, then on List All.
- In the @ Function box, scroll until you see MAX. Click on MAX and then click on the **OK** button.
- Highlight cells B12 to F12, then click on the tick icon.
- Do the same with cell D18, this time choosing MIN in the @ Function dialogue box.
- Finally, check that you are satisfied with the formats of all numbers, column widths, display style and accuracy before going any further.
- Save your file again before moving on to create a graph.

—— 4.6 Creating a bar chart ——

This section shows how to produce from the spreadsheet a chart that shows the proportions of each vehicle type sold. All the work in this section of the chapter will be carried out using the Tools option from the menu bar.

The basic order of activities that you will need to go through to produce a graph is as follows:

1 Highlight the area of the spreadsheet to be graphed.
2 Create the graph.
3 Define the ranges that are to make up the graph.
4 Select a graph type.

In this first example, you will generate a Bar graph that will show units sold for each vehicle type.

- Highlight the range B12..F12 which are the numbers of vehicle types sold, the data to be plotted on the graph.
- Click on Tools, then Chart.
- The mouse pointer will change to a small graphics icon. Point this near the top corner of your spreadsheet and click the left mouse button.
- Now position your mouse pointer over the bottom right corner of the graph area created. The pointer will turn into a white cross. Holding down the left mouse button, drag the chart area downwards and right to create a larger graph.

Screen dump 4.5 illustrates the graph created and how it is being 'stretched' so that it appears bigger on the screen. Although the graph is covering the spreadsheet table, it will not cause any loss of data.

Such graphs are created as floating objects, in that they appear to *float* over the spreadsheet without affecting the spreadsheet contents underneath them. Later you will be shown how to temporarily remove such objects from vision, thereby revealing all the spreadsheet contents.

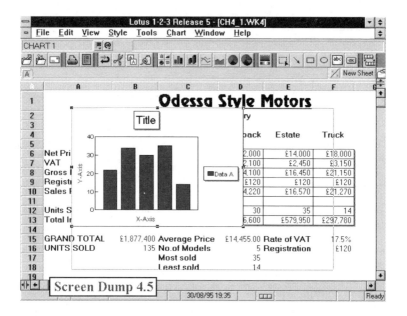

Your next goal will be to define the precise ranges that are to make up the graph. Look at the top of the screen and you will see that you now have a different menu bar. You also have a new set of SmartIcons.

• Familiarise yourself with the new screen.
• Click on Chart, then select Ranges.

The X-axis will always appear along the bottom of the bar chart unless you specify otherwise. The data ranges will appear on the left of the chart as a vertical axis. The data range was identified as the range B12 to F12 when it was highlighted prior to creating the chart. What is now required is to specify the fact that the vertical axis is

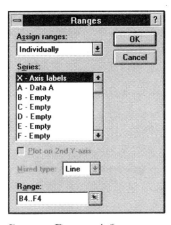

Screen Dump 4.6

plotting the Type of Motor vehicle, which is needed along the X-axis. The Number of Units Sold will later need to appear down the vertical (or Y) axis.

This now leaves you with a dialogue box to complete in order to define the X-axis range. **Screen dump 4.6** shows the kind of screen you will be given. The X range has been defined as B4..F4.

- Click on X-axis labels in the Series box.
- Now click on the Range box and enter the range value B4..F4.
- Click on the **OK** button and observe what has now been achieved.

If you had not highlighted the range B12 to F12 before creating the bar chart, then defining the ranges for both X and Y could have been done at this stage. Release 5, however, will prompt you automatically for the data ranges.

You will now have a 2-D bar chart. The next stage will be to alter this chart to a 3-D bar chart.

- Click on Chart then select Type.

Screen dump 4.7 shows that you have a selection of graph types to choose from in the Types box. Each type will then activate a collection of icons. For the purpose of this section of the chapter you should start with the 3-D bar chart because this is the simplest.

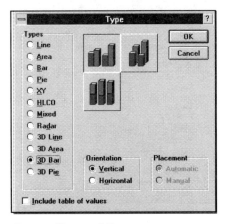

Screen Dump 4.7

Many other graph types will not be appropriate for this kind of spreadsheet example. Chapter 8 will give you the chance to work with many of the other graph types and with different kinds of data that are more appropriate.

As an alternative to this you can click your mouse button on the 3-D bar graph SmartIcon.

Screen dump 4.8 shows the result you should get.

It was suggested earlier that if you change your data, in this case the number of units sold, then the graph would change to match the new data. It is now worth doing this to see the effect.

The first problem to resolve is to reveal the part of the spreadsheet that shows the number of units sold.

- Click on Ⅴiew then select Set View Ⲣreferences and de-activate the Chart, drawings and pictures box by removing the small 'x' beside it.
- Now click on **OK**. This will hide the chart from view.
- Now change the number of units sold in row 12:

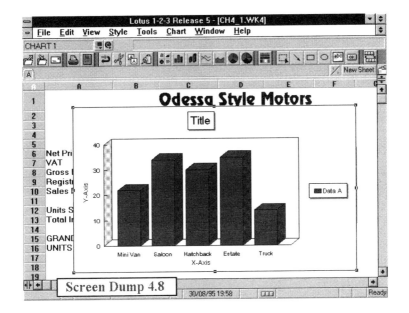

Screen Dump 4.8

Cell	Units sold
B12	51
C12	101
D12	14
E12	31
F12	62

- Now restore the graph by clicking on <u>V</u>iew then select Set View Preferences and activate the Chart, drawings and pictures. Then click on the **OK** button.

The graph is technically sound, but to make it more professional you can add labels and a title.

- Click on the graph area. Then double click on the Title box in the graph. You will see the Headings dialogue box.
- Type into two boxes:

Line 1 (the title):   ODESSA STYLE MOTORS
Line 2 (the subtitle):   Sales for January
then click on the **OK** button.

Next you should label the axes appropriately, noting that the horizontal axis is the X-axis and the vertical the Y-axis.

● Click on the words X-axis in the graph. Square boxes will appear in the four corners. Double click the mouse and you will see the X-axis dialogue box. The A<u>x</u>is title box will be highlighted, so double click on the box and type in the words: Vehicle Type, then click on the **OK** button.

● Click on the words Y-axis in the graph, then double click the mouse. The Y-axis dialogue box will appear. Double click on the A<u>x</u>is title box and type in the words: Number of Units Sold, then click on the **OK** button.

● Finally, double click on the Data A box. You want to delete this, so click on the <u>L</u>egend entry box and press **Delete** until the box is clear of text. Then click on the **OK** button.

Screen dump 4.9 shows the graph with the appropriate titles and labels on the axes.

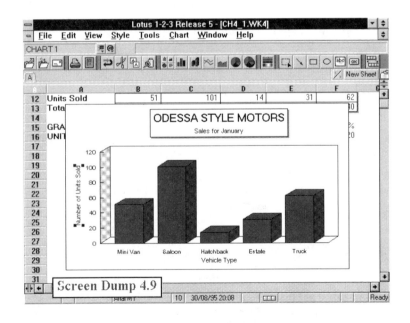

Screen Dump 4.9

Finally, you will need to name your graph for later use.

• Click on <u>C</u>hart, then <u>N</u>ame. You will see that the Name dialogue box will have given your graph or bar chart the default name CHART 1. Click on the <u>C</u>hart name box and type in the name ODESSA.

In Chapter 8 you will create a collection of graphs, all in the same spreadsheet. Lotus 1-2-3 allows you to have many graphs defined in a spreadsheet. It distinguishes between the different graphs by giving each one a unique name. These 'named' graphs will, therefore, become part of the spreadsheet when it is saved or opened.

—— 4.7 Changing the graph type ——

Changing the graph is simple.

• Click on the three-dimensional Pie Chart SmartIcon.

Screen dump 4.10 shows a resulting pie chart.

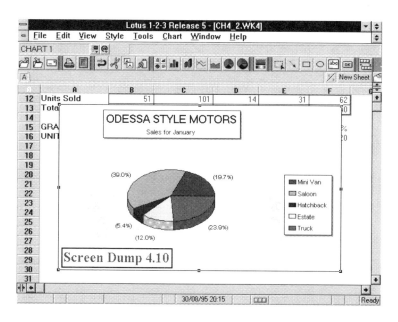

The pie chart shows the same data as the bar chart but this time the segments give the proportion of total sales. Observe that Lotus 1-2-3 shows against each segment the percentage each segment represents of the whole. Add these percentages together to get 100%.

In both graphs, Lotus 1-2-3 scales up the elements to fill up a reasonable proportion of the screen. You can control this yourself, and this will be covered in Chapter 8.

Experiment with the other SmartIcons; many of them, however, will not be appropriate. Further graph types will be developed in Chapter 8 along with many other facilities that are available with the Lotus 1-2-3 graphics.

— 4.8 Customising the spreadsheet —

Up to now you can see either your graph or your spreadsheet, but not both. In this section you will move ranges around the spreadsheet leaving a suitable place to position your graph. You will also reduce the size of the graph and move it to the new position. In doing so, you will see how Lotus 1-2-3 allows you to scale down your graph so that it is a better size to appear on your spreadsheet and for subsequent printing.

At this stage it is worth looking at some of the options available for altering the appearance of your graph.

- Click on the chart area to make the chart area active.
- Now click on the right mouse button to reveal a small menu.
- Click on Lines & Color from this menu.

If you look at **Screen dump 4.11** you will see that you now have the option of altering the interior of your chart, the edges and the frame.

- Click on the Designer Frame option and select a frame and frame colour that appeals to you.
- Experiment with some of the other options.
- Click on the **OK** button and inspect your work. If it is not suitable, then return to the Lines & Color box and make the necessary alterations. Do not concern yourself about getting an exact match to those in the screen dumps.

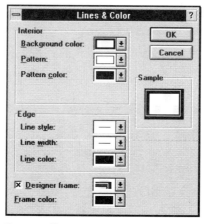

Screen Dump 4.11

Your next task will be to position the graph in the spreadsheet so that it will print neatly. To do this you will move ranges from the spreadsheet to make a space for the graph.

● Highlight cells C15 to D18.
● Now position the mouse pointer on the edge of the highlighted range so that a small hand appears.
● With the hand on the screen, hold down the left mouse button. The fist clenches to indicate you have grabbed the cell. Slowly drag the entire block to appear under 'Units Sold' in cells A16 to B16 and let go of the mouse button.

Not only have all cell contents been preserved, but the cells used in the formulae have been changed to compensate for the moved cell locations.

● Now move cells E15 to F16 in the same way, to fit under 'Least Sold' in cells A20 to B20.

Not only have the formulae in the cells you have moved been preserved, but the formulae elsewhere in the spreadsheet have been altered to allow for the change in location.

Now to move the graph.

- Click on the graph area, hold down the left mouse button, and move the entire chart so that its top left corner is positioned at cell C15.
- Resize the chart to fit the page best.

The graph should now be below the table similar to that shown in **Screen dump 4.12**.

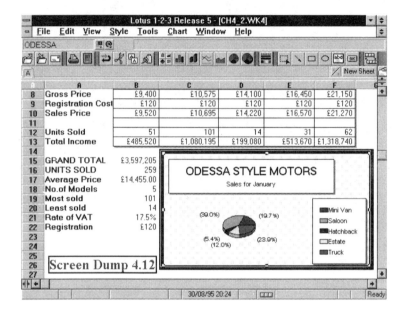

To finish this chapter, you will preview the page to be printed and then print it.

- Click on the Print Preview SmartIcon, then click on Current <u>W</u>orksheet in the Preview box, and click on the **OK** button.

Screen dump 4.13 illustrates what you should see as a preview and is also what will appear on the printout. When you first see this screen, a small spy glass appears on the screen that is controlled using the mouse. By positioning your mouse over the top part of the image and clicking it, you can zoom in to get a closer look at what will be printed. **Screen dump 4.13** illustrates this effect of zooming in closer.

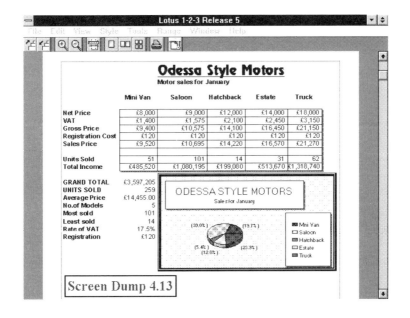

Screen Dump 4.13

- Make sure there is paper in your printer and the printer is switched on, and click on the print SmartIcon to activate the print dialogue box.
- Click on the **OK** button to start the printing.

———— 4.9 Chapter summary ————

In this chapter you have concentrated on some of the many statistical functions and formulae available in Lotus 1-2-3 and developed a few of the graph formats available. In particular you have:

- covered more work on text, values, formulae and function entries to cells.
- altered the style and presentation of the spreadsheet.

- copied ranges of cells with absolute and relative formula contents.
- produced a graph.
- labelled the graph.
- generated different graphs.
- moved ranges of cells around your spreadsheet.
- positioned a graph in the spreadsheet.

5

STYLE AND PRESENTATION

5.1 Aims of this chapter

This chapter concentrates on a number of issues regarding the set up of your spreadsheet and how to present your data in a form that is appropriate to the problem in hand. It will also explain the good practice of naming areas of your spreadsheet.

The first part of the chapter is based on a stock system set out in tabular form showing data in a number of different formats.

The second part of the chapter is based on a sales report showing sales and profit figures in a simple table with a chart and a significant amount of text. The text will be manipulated in a way similar to a word processor and will show you how you can import text from a word processing package.

5.2 Styles for data

As a starting point examine the spreadsheet in **Screen dump 5.1**, which lists items of stock showing Stock Code, Description, Number in stock, Cost Price and Selling Price.

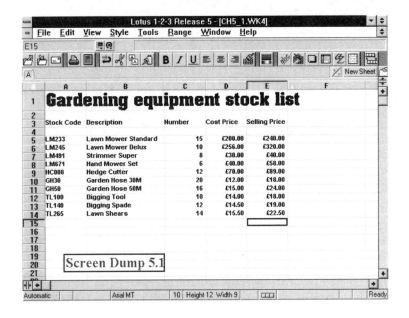

Screen Dump 5.1

- In order to get started, type in the data in **Screen dump 5.1** in a new spreadsheet.
- Click on the white letter A in the left-hand side of the row headings at the top of the column numbers. This will highlight the entire spreadsheet. In the status line, click on the 12, the default font size, and then click on 10, to make all the characters in the spreadsheet smaller.
- If you have not already done so, widen column B by clicking on the dividing line between column headings B and C and pulling the columns apart.
- Give the title 'Gardening equipment stock list' a more prominent size and face. Highlight the range that contains the heading, then click on Arial in the bottom line and choose a different face. When you have done this, click on the number 10 in the bottom status line and increase the size of the font.

- The numbers in columns D and E are Currency. Highlight cells D5 to E14, click the right mouse button, then select Number Format.
- From the Number Format dialogue box select the Currency option and set the numbers to 2 decimal places.
- Click on the date and time indicator on the status line to give details about the size of the cell the pointer is in.

In this section and the next, you will examine in more detail some of the other formats available in Lotus 1-2-3. You now have enough information to type in to the spreadsheet stock details about value and possible profit.

- Click on cell F3 and enter the label Stock Value.
- Now click on cell F5 and enter the formula +C5*D5.

The formula in cell F5 multiplies the Stock Quantity with the Cost Price. Do not copy this formula yet, as you will do that later.

- Click on cell G3 and type in the label Unit Profit.
- Now click on cell G5 and type in formula +E5-D5.

The formula in cell G5 subtracts Cost Price from Selling Price to give the Unit Profit. Again, do not copy this formula yet.

- Click on cell H3 and type in the label Gross Profit.
- Now click on cell H5 and type in the formula +C5*G5.

The formula in cell H5 multiplies the Stock Quantity with the Unit Profit to give the Gross Profit per line.

- Format the range F5 to H5 as currency, to 2 decimal places.

At this stage, you now have three formulae that can be copied down the spreadsheet in one operation.

- Highlight the range F5 to H5.
- With your arrow on the highlighted cells, click the right mouse button and select Copy to copy the formulae to the Clipboard (or click on Edit in the menu bar, then Copy).
- Highlight the destination range F6 to H14.
- With your arrow on the highlighted cells, click the right mouse button, then select Paste to copy the formulae from the Clipboard to the highlighted range.

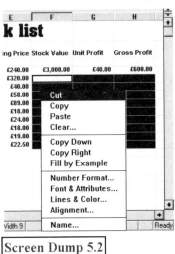

Screen Dump 5.2

Screen dump 5.2 shows this destination range highlighted with the mouse-generated menu that is used to paste the Clipboard contents. Notice how the formats have also been copied.

- Click on cell E10, type in 10 and press **Enter**. Observe how the Unit Profit appears in brackets to indicate a loss and how the formats have remained as currency.

5.3 Date formats

At this stage your spreadsheet should be fairly full. The next stage is to type in a date when the stock was received. You will also create a column to store the number of days the last stock has been held. In doing this you will learn a little about the Lotus 1-2-3 date function and how it can be used.

The date function appears in the format @DATE(95,6,22) where:

95 is the year 1995
6 is the 6th month: June
22 is the day in the month.

You are able to enter a date into a cell but you will not see it appear in an immediately recognisable format, as you will now find out.

- Click on cell I3 and enter the label Last and in cell I4 the label Delivery.
- Now Click on cell I5 and enter the date function with a date as @DATE(95,6,19).

What will appear in the cell is the number 34869. This is the number of days between 1 January 1900 and the date that was entered (19 June 1995). This may seem odd at first, but it will allow you to perform some useful calculations. However, to make sense of it you will need to alter its format.

- Highlight the whole range where the dates are to appear, i.e., cells I5 to I14.
- With your arrow on the highlighted cells, click on the right mouse button, and select the Number Format option.
- Click on the Dates option in the Format box.

Screen dump 5.3 shows the Number Format dialogue box with Dates selection. Lotus 1-2-3 gives you a selection of Date formats to choose from. The Sample panel in this dialogue box illustrates how the date will appear.

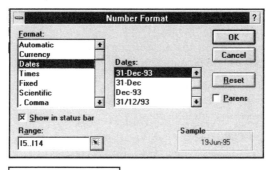

Screen Dump 5.3

- Click on the 31-Dec-93 format and then click on the **OK** button.

Although only the one cell has an actual date in it, Lotus 1-2-3 allows you to prepare in advance the cell format for future input.

Type in the following dates in their respective cells:

Cell   Date

I6	@DATE(95,6,20)
I7	@DATE(95,6,10)
I8	@DATE(95,6,15)
I9	@DATE(95,6,20)
I10	@DATE(95,6,10)
I11	@DATE(95,6,15)
I12	@DATE(95,6,20)
I13	@DATE(95,6,10)
I14	@DATE(95,6,15)

As you enter these dates you should see the date format you requested appear.

Column J will hold the number of days between the date of the last delivery and the current date. What you need, therefore, is a facility whereby the computer can calculate this for you. the function that will allow this is @TODAY.

- Click on cell A16 and type in the label Date.
- Now click on cell B16 and type in @TODAY.
- Now format the cell with the date option, as before.

Providing your computer has the correct date and time set, you should now have today's date. If the date is wrong, then enter today's date in the cell, using the date function. The benefit of the TODAY function over the DATE function is that if you return to the spreadsheet on another day, the date is altered automatically.

You now have the facility to enter the days lapsed between a delivery date and today for each item of stock.

- Click on cell J3 and type in label Days and in J4 the label Lapsed.
- Click on cell J5 and type in the formula +b16-I5.

This calculates the number of days from today to the date of the last delivery. Notice also how the cell location B16 in the formula has been set as absolute.

- Now copy the formula in cell J3 to the cells J6 to J14.

At this stage you should have a spreadsheet similar to that of **Screen dump 5.4**.

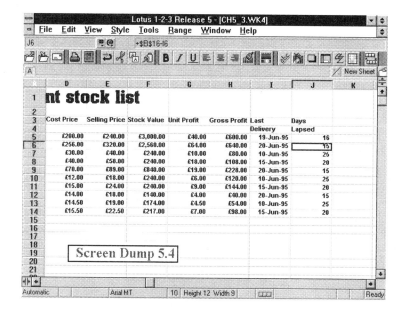

5.4 Naming ranges

This section will show you how you can give a range of cells a distinct name rather than identifying it by its cells. It is much easier to remember the name of a range rather than the coordinates of a range. It is also a useful way of documenting what is on your spreadsheet.

- Highlight cells F5 to F14.
- With your arrow on the highlighted cells, click on the right mouse button, and select Name.
- In the Name dialogue box, type in Stock Value and click on the **OK** button.
- Now click on cell F16 and type in the formula that will calculate the sum: @SUM(Stock Value).

Instead of using the range references in the formula, you were able to use the range name. This will make a spreadsheet much easier to follow if you return to it at a later stage and examine the formulae.

- Highlight cells G5 to G14.
- Give the range the title Unit Profit.

You will notice that the Existing named ranges panel contains a list of range names already in existence; these are automatically written in upper case despite the fact that you may have typed them in upper and lower case. You cannot have two ranges with the same name.

- Highlight cells H5 to H14.
- Give the range the title Gross Profit.
- Now click on cell H16 and type in the formula to calculate the sum: @SUM(Gross Profit).
- Highlight cells J5 to J14.
- Give the range the title Days Lapsed.

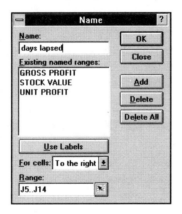

Screen Dump 5.5

Screen dump 5.5 shows the screen you should have seen when creating or selecting a named range.

You now have a collection of these range names and it is always a good idea to keep a list of them somewhere. Fortunately, Lotus 1-2-3 can do this for you.

- Click on Range, then Name. Highlight the range name DAYS LAPSED in the Existing named ranges box.

- Now click on the Use Labels button, then click on the **OK** button.

When you return to the spreadsheet the selected range remains highlighted. This can be particularly useful when your spreadsheet becomes large.

As a final illustration of their use, do the following:

- Click on cell E17, type in the label Averages, and in cell G17 the function @AVG(Unit Profit).
- Click on cell J17 and type in the function @AVG(Days Lapsed).
- Format the range F16 to H17 to currency as before.
- Format cell J17 to Number Format Fixed, to 0 decimal places.

—— 5.5 Summarising the formats ——

- Highlight cells A3 to J4. Click on Style, then Alignment.
- In the horizontal box, click on Centre and then click on the **OK** button.

You can align data within a cell or across the columns of a range. Select the Range and then click on the appropriate box. Under Horizontal you have the following:

General	Aligns labels to the left and values to the right.
Left	Aligns data to the left.
Right	Aligns data to the right.
Centre	Centres data.
Evenly spaced	Stretches data within the cell by expanding the spaces between letters and words.
Across columns	For ranges only: aligns data in the leftmost cell over the columns within the range, according to your selection under Horizontal.

There are also SmartIcons that will centre, right align and left align data highlighted in cells or ranges.

You have now made use of most of the Number Format options from the Style pull-down menu. The following are available:

Fixed	Displays numbers to a specified number of decimal places, a minus sign for negatives, and a leading zero for decimal values.

Scientific	Numbers are displayed in the form of for example, 4.733E-2. This scientific form is similar to that available on most calculators.
Currency	Currency symbols are used as prefix or suffix, depending how you have determined it. Thousands are separated with commas. Negative numbers are bracketed.
Comma	Commas are used to separate thousands. Negative numbers are bracketed.
General	The default format is set: numbers are displayed with a minus sign for negatives, no thousand separators and no trailing zeros to the right of the decimal point.
+/-	This converts numbers to rows of + (plus) or (–) minus. The number 5 would be displayed as +++++ while –3 would appear as – – – –.
Percent	This multiplies a stored number by 100, sets it to a specified number of decimal places and places a % sign after it.
Text	This displays the cell formulae and functions rather than their computed value.
Hidden	This allows you to hide cell contents from display without actually removing them from the spreadsheet.
Automatic	If you type in, say $1000, Lotus 1-2-3 assigns the Currency format; if you type 8/25/95, it assigns a date format.
Label	Displays new entries as labels by automatically adding label-prefix character that corresponds to the alignment set on Style Worksheet Defaults. Displays existing numbers in General format.

There then follows a set of Date formats and then a set of Time formats.

—— 5.6 Protecting ranges of cells ——

This final section dealing with your current spreadsheet will show you how to protect ranges of cells from being written over. The process is as follows:

1 Define the range(s) that you wish to write on, called unprotected areas.
2 Set the worksheet as Sealed, where only unprotected parts can be written on.

3 Set a password, so that only someone knowing the password can reverse the process.

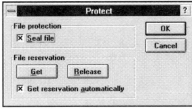

Screen Dump 5.6

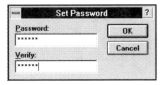

Screen dump 5.6 shows the three dialogue boxes that match the three stages listed above. You will need to refer back to this as you proceed. The first stage is to decide which areas of the spreadsheet you do wish to write to.

• Highlight cells C5 to H14.
• Click on Style, then Protection.
• Click on the keep data unprotected box as shown in the top part of **Screen dump 5.6**.
• Click on the **OK** button.

You have now requested Lotus 1-2-3 to allow you to write to any cell in this range once the file has been Sealed. For the second stage you need to Seal the file.

• Click on File, then click on Protect.
• Click on Seal file, in the File protection box as shown in the middle of **Screen dump 5.6**, then click on the **OK** button.

For the third stage, you will be asked for a password. As you enter the password an asterisk will appear for each character, thereby concealing what you are entering. The bottom part of **Screen dump 5.6** shows this. The purpose is to ensure that no one can see your password being entered. In addition to the password, you have to put exactly the same text into the Verify box. If they differ in the slightest way, Lotus 1-2-3 will not seal the file.

- Type in the letters GARDEN into the Password box (all in capitals).
- Type in the letters GARDEN into the Verify box and click on the **OK** button.

The cells that are unprotected will appear in blue while the text in black cannot be written to.

- Now try and alter one of the cells in black.

The only real problem you could have here is forgetting your password.

To release the protection you would click on File, then Protect. However, Lotus 1-2-3 will ask for your password before it unseals the file for you.

—————— 5.7 Presenting text ——————

This second part of the chapter looks at dealing with text in more detail and examines some of the presentation qualities available in the Lotus 1-2-3 package. The concentration is very much on visual appearance.

In a new spreadsheet you will enter details concerning an improvement in sales with the following sections:

> heading
> a box of text
> a graph
> a table

First, the heading:

- In cell A1 type: Bumper Sales Year and Profits.
- Now use the font and size buttons to enhance this heading, and then underline it.

Typing in the text will prove a little more interesting. You will type in just two cells to start with and then get Lotus 1-2-3 to rearrange it in a range of cells. Observe what appears in **Screen dump 5.7**.

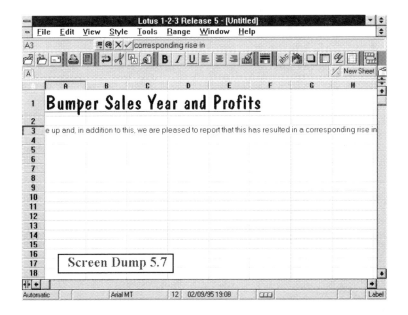

Screen Dump 5.7

The text typed into cell A3 is much longer than can appear on one line and appears to go off the screen. You can enter up to 256 characters in a single line.

● Type in the following text in cell A3 remembering not to press **Enter**:

As shown in the graph, we are pleased to report a significant increase in our sales for the last year. As you can see from the graph, sales are up and, in addition to this, we are pleased to report that this has resulted in a corresponding rise in

Note how the text is now off the screen.

● Type in the following text in cell A4 as you did in cell A3:

profits. We are also pleased to report that this rise over the last year is expected to continue into next year and even into the foreseeable future.

You will now ask Lotus to take this text and reformat it into a range of cells to make all the text visible.

Highlight cells A3 to D13.

You will now activate a different menu known as the *Classic menu*. Follow the next three steps:

- Activate the classic menu with the / (forward slash) key.
- Select Justify from the menu by pressing the **J** key.

The text will now have been reformatted into this range and no text should go over this specified range. You will also notice that the single range defined must contain the text as well as being the area you want the text displayed. This can be particularly helpful when you want, for example, to reformat text that takes up a full screen down one side of the spreadsheet. This will allow you to have columns of text similar to that of newspapers.

—— 5.8 Search & replace text ——

If you use a word processing package, then you will already be familiar with this facility. Lotus 1-2-3 can scan through a range of text searching for a word (or string of characters) and if necessary replace it. As an example get Lotus 1-2-3 to replace the word 'report' with 'announce'.

- Highlight cells A3 to D11.
- Click on Range, then Name, type article in the Name box, then click on the **OK** button.

This names that part of the spreadsheet where the text is stored. It can be referenced later.

- Click on Edit, Find & Replace.

You will see a series of boxes in the Find & Replace dialogue box.

- Type in ARTICLE in the Selected range box to indicate where the text is on the spreadsheet.
- In the Search for box type in report.
- In the Replace with box type in announce.
- The Include panel should be set to Both.

At this point you will see a screen as shown in the top part of **Screen dump 5.8**.

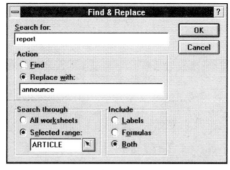

Screen Dump 5.8

● Click on the **OK** button.

A set of buttons, as shown in the lower part of **Screen dump 5.8**, on the screen indicate one of three actions that can now be taken:

Find Next: Highlights the first occurrence of 'report' without replacing the current occurrence.

Replace Locates the first occurrence of the string 'report' and replaces it with 'announce'.

Replace All Replaces all occurrences of 'report' with 'announce' in the specified range, then returns to the Ready mode.

● Click on Replace All.

You will now be able to observe that all occurrences of 'report' have been replaced with 'announce'.

You can use this facility simply to locate words in a long piece of text without replacing anything. Being able to search for text in this fashion will be of particular use if you have a very large amount of text stored in your spreadsheet.

5.9 Inserting graphs into a spreadsheet

• Take a look at **Screen dump 5.9** to see what is to be achieved next.

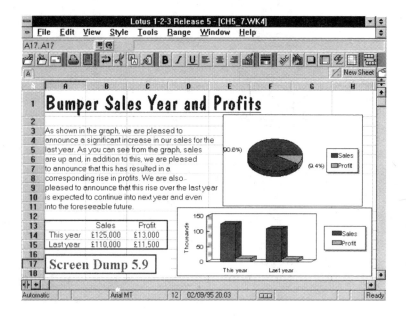

Type in the table that appears in the bottom left-hand corner.

Cell	Data
A14	This year
A15	Last year
B13	Sales
C13	Profit
B14	125000
B15	110000
C14	13000
C15	11500

• Format the four numeric values to currency, with zero decimal places. Centre the data in all 8 cells.

- Highlight cells A13 to C15 and, with the Lines & Color option, give the range a thick line border.

At this stage you have the text and tables all nicely boxed up.

You will produce two graphs: a pie chart showing the percentages of Sales and Profits for the current year; a bar chart showing a Sales and Profit comparison for this year and last year. Remember, you can have as many graphs/charts open at any one time as you want.

Pie chart

- Highlight cells A13 to C14.
- Click on Tools, then Chart.
- Move the pointer to the area of the spreadsheet to the right of the text. Press down the right mouse button and size the chart to take up the area shown in **Screen dump 5.9**.
- Click on the 3-D Pie Chart SmartIcon.
- Click on the Title in the graph area and press the **Delete** key on your keyboard.

Bar chart

- Highlight cells A14 to C15.
- Click on Tools, then Chart.
- Move the pointer to the area of the spreadsheet below the Pie Chart. Press down the right mouse button and size the chart to take up the area shown in **Screen dump 5.9**.
- Click on the 3-D Bar Chart SmartIcon.
- Click on the X-axis label that appears on the bar chart, then press the **Delete** key on your keyboard. Repeat this for the Y-axis label that also appears on the bar chart.

If you compare what you have now with **Screen dump 5.9**, you will see a difference. Although the bar chart as it stands has some meaning, you will now alter the ranges to show a comparison of the two Sales figures and the two Profit figures.

- Click on Chart, then Legend.
- In the Legend Dialogue box click on A-This year in the Series box, then highlight the Legend entry box.

- Move the pointer to the spreadsheet, highlight cells B13 to B15, then click on the **OK** button. Use **Screen dump 5.10** to check the dialogue box.
- Again, click on Chart, then Legend.

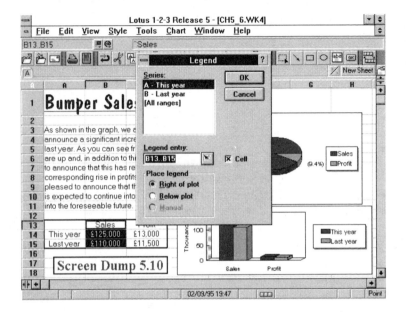

- In the Legend Dialogue box click on B-Last year in the Series box, then highlight the Legend entry box.
- Move the pointer to the spreadsheet, highlight cells C13 to C15, then click on the **OK** button.
- Click on Chart, then Ranges.
- In the Ranges dialogue box click on X-axis labels in the Series box, then highlight the Range entry box.
- Move the pointer to the spreadsheet and highlight cells A14 to A15, then click on the **OK** button.
- Again, click on Chart, then Ranges.
- In the Ranges dialogue box click on A-Sales in the Series box, then highlight the Range entry box.
- Move the pointer to the spreadsheet and highlight cells B14 to B15, then click on the **OK** button.

- Again, click on Chart, then Ranges.
- In the Ranges dialogue box click on B-Profit in the Series box, then highlight the Range entry box.
- Move the pointer on to the spreadsheet and highlight cells C14 to C15, then click on the **OK** button.
- Now rearrange the boxes to make an attractive print out.
- Save the file, and print the results.

To finish this chapter, you should also try changing the data in cells B14 to C15 to see how the changes in the data affect the two graphs.

——— 5.10 Chapter summary ———

It is worth noting that spreadsheets are often set up by people experienced in this area but are operated by others who want to look at the data and carry out simple operations. Good presentation is very important if someone with limited skills in spreadsheet handling is going to extract information from them. If you return to spreadsheets you have designed after a long absence, you may be unable to find your way around if they are badly presented and muddled. Therefore, presentation and organisation, central themes of this chapter, are all important.

In this chapter you have:

- altered cell widths to fit the data in them.
- named and used ranges as both a way of better documentation and a more efficient way of working with ranges.
- had more practice with formatting ranges of cells.
- used the Lotus 1-2-3 date function for display and calculations.
- protected ranges of data from being written over.
- written and manipulated text boxes.
- used search and replace.
- created different kinds of graphs.
- produced attractively presented text, data and graphs.

6

DATES AND
DECISIONS

6.1 Aims of this chapter

This chapter further develops the use of dates, building up formulae and moving cell contents around the spreadsheet. It also looks at Lotus 1-2-3's ability to ask questions and give results based on these questions. The chapter does this with two examples, the first trading in shares and the second a monthly sales analysis.

6.2 More practice with formats

This first example is designed to show you more about writing formulae, manipulating dates, moving ranges and inserting rows and columns.

Screen dump 6.5 is what you are aiming for (note the three parts). You will set it up in a slightly different way across the screen so that you can move things around for practice.

- Start with a blank spreadsheet and type in a company title, R Enterprises will do, but use any company name you wish.
- Next, type in identification labels. Use your mouse to speed things up.

  Cell   Type in

  D3   Commission Rate

A4	Purchase
A6	Date
B6	Shares
C6	Price
D6	Commission
E6	Cost

- Widen column D so that the label Commission is fully visible.
- Type in cell F3 the value 3%. For Release 4 users, the number 0.03 may appear. If this is so, format it to per cent to zero decimal places.
- Centre the labels in cells A6 to E6.

Next you will use the Lotus 1-2-3 drawing facilities to draw a line from cell A5 to cell E5. What will be created is a floating object that can be moved around the spreadsheet in a similar way to charts. The object appears on the spreadsheet but will not endanger any data wherever it is positioned.

- Click on Tools, then Draw, then Line.

At this stage you should have a spreadsheet looking similar to that depicted in **screen dump 6.1**.

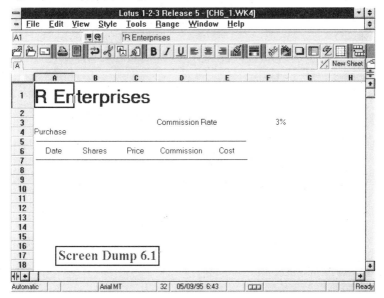

— 6.3 More on manipulating dates —

Begin by typing in the purchase date, 20 October 1995. You could type in the date as a label by prefixing it with an apostrophe. However, in this exercise, you will require the computer to perform some arithmetic on this date and so the entry must be typed in as a function similar to that performed in Chapter 5.

- Click on cell A8 and type in @DATE(95,10,20), that is Year, Month, Day.

The number that appears in the cell, if calculated manually, would tell you that this is the number of days that have lapsed between the date typed in and 1 January 1900. At this stage format this column as dates.

- Highlight cells A8 to A10.
- With the mouse pointer over this highlighted area, click the left mouse button and, from the menu that appears, click on Number Format option.
- In the Format box in the Number Format dialogue box, click on date and select the 31-Dec-93 format, then click on the **OK** button.

Remember, Lotus 1-2-3 allows you to format cells before you type in data.

- Click on cell B8 and type in 100 - the number of shares purchased.
- Click on cell C8 and type in 0.5 (i.e. 50 pence or cents) – the share price.
- Now format the cells C8 to E10 as currency, to two places of decimals.
- Click on cell D8 and type in the formula +B8*C8*$F$3.

The formula in cell D8 contains an absolute cell reference F3. Remember, when this formula is copied, all cell references with a dollar sign placed in front of them will not alter, while others will change relative to the cell they are copied to.

You will see the figure £1.50 in cell D8.

- Click on cell E8 and type in the formula +B8*C8+D8.

The formula in cell E8 multiplies the number of shares by the price per share and then adds the commission to this to give the final cost of this transaction.

- Now type in the next two rows of data:

  In Cell   Type in

  A9   @DATE(95,12,6)
  B9   500
  C9   1.5 [this will appear as £1.50]
  A10   @DATE(94,8,18)
  B10   150
  C10   1 [this will appear as £1.00]

- Highlight cells D8 to E10.
- With the pointer on the highlighted cells, click the left mouse button and then click on the Copy Down option from the menu that appears.
- Save the spreadsheet with the name HST1.

At this stage, you should have something similar to **Screen dump 6.2**.

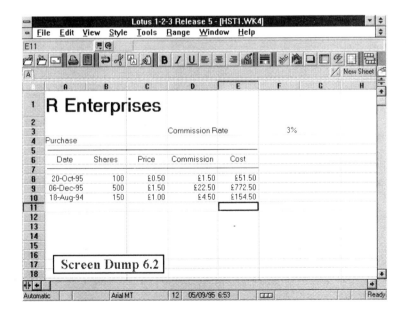

Regular saving of your work at intervals is recommended. Situations do arise when you are drawn away from your computer and the system is shut down by someone else leaving all your efforts as lost. You may also experience power failures or make a silly mistake that causes your work to be lost. If you save your work every 15 minutes, for example, you need only go back 15 minutes if your spreadsheet is inadvertently lost.

Correcting mistakes

If you do make a mistake, click on the Undo SmartIcon and your last action will be 'undone'.

— 6. 4 Copying and moving ranges —

This section will deal with expanding the spreadsheet further to include details about the sale of these shares at a later date. It requires the movement of ranges. As the sales information will be similar to purchase information, it seems common sense to take advantage of this fact.

- Highlight the cells A4 to E10.
- Click on Range, then Name, then name the range PURCHASE.
- Highlight cells A4 to E10.
- Position the mouse pointer on the edge so the small hand shows. Hold down the **Ctrl** and left mouse button at the same time, and drag a copy of the block of cells to start at cell F4. Release 5 users will see a plus sign appear on the hand.

This is a rather useful alternative to the Copy and Paste facilities.

Take note now of how Lotus 1-2-3 has copied the range. It assumes that F4 is the top left cell of the range copied in the same way as A4 is of the source range. In order to be consistent in naming ranges, it should be done for this next range.

- If cells F4 to J10 are not still highlighted, then Highlight them now.
- Click on the left mouse button while the pointer is over the range to get a menu.
- Now click on Name, then name the range SALE.

For now, the entire spreadsheet will not be visible on the screen and the range Sale will be wrongly labelled. As a further demonstration of the benefits of naming ranges, try the following:

- Go to cell A1 by pressing your **Home** key on the keyboard.
- Now press function key **F5**, which is the 'go to' key.
- Instead of typing in a cell reference, click on SALE and then click on the **OK** button.

This takes you to cell F4, the top left part of the range. Next you should amend the details in this range.

- Type in a new label for cell F4: Sale; and change the label in cell J6 from Cost to Amount.
- Centre the label in cell J6.
- In cell F8 type @DATE(95,12,28).

The correct date format (i.e. 28-Dec-95) should now appear because the range you copied from had this cell formatted for the date format.

- Click on cell G8 and type in 90, the number of shares, and click on cell H8 and type in 0.84, the price of shares.

The broker's commission in cell I8 has automatically been calculated for you. Observe the formula in this cell and see how the reference point to the commission rate (which is stored in cell F3) is preserved because of its absolute status in the formula. It should become + G8*H8*$F$3.

- Click on cell F3 and type in the commission rate of 5%.

This will change the commissions in both Purchase and Sale ranges.

- Work out a formula for cell J8 to calculate the amount received from the share sale. If you do not arrive at the figure in the cell then read on.
- The formula is +G8*H8-I8 which is the price per share multiplied by the number sold, less the commission.
- Now type in next two rows of data to replace the figures copied from cells A8 to B10:

In Cell Type in

F9   @DATE(95,12,28)
G9   300
H9   1.45

F10   @DATE(96,1,15)
G10   100
H10   1.4

- Now copy the cells formula in I8 and J8 to cells I9 to J10.

At this stage you should have your Sale range as in **Screen dump 6.3**.

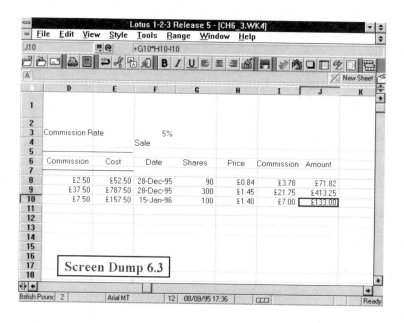

Screen Dump 6.3

The active area of your spreadsheet, as shown in **Screen dump 6.3**, now goes further to the right than your screen allows you to see and you will have to move around your spreadsheet to see everything. The range named 'Sales' will be moved below the range named 'Purchase' later on.

This is now a useful time to practise skipping around.

- Click on cell A5, press the **End** key on your keyboard and then the **Right Arrow** key once. This moves the cell pointer to cell J5, the furthest cell to the right with any data in it.
- Press the **Home** key to get to cell A1. Now press **End** followed by the **Down Arrow**. This will take you to the next cell down that contains any data.

However much planning is done there is often a need to change the design of a spreadsheet. There are many ways of shunting things around. For now you will concentrate on the move command to bring the Sale range down below the Purchase range allowing the data on the spreadsheet to be more easily observed. **Screen dump 6.4** shows the effect this will have, leaving all data visible without you needing to move out of any area of the spreadsheet or creating a window.

- Press the **F5** function, 'go to' and click on the SALE name. Click on **OK** to see the range highlighted.
- Position the mouse pointer to the edge of the highlighted range until an open hand appears.
- Drag the range so that the top left corner is at cell A12 and release your mouse button.

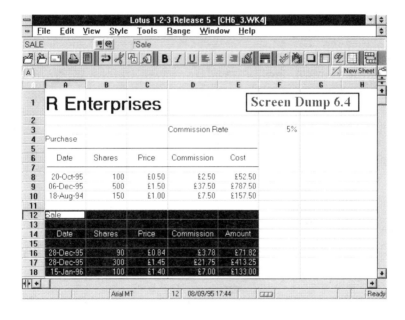

An alternative to this would have been to highlight the range you want moved and then, from the Edit pull down menu click on Cut (or click on the Cut SmartIcon). You would then move the cell pointer to where you want the contents situated and, from the Edit pull down menu again, click on *P*aste (or click on the Paste SmartIcon).

This method of Cut & Paste may prove to be a better method if you are not too clear where you want the range of cells moved to in the first instance.

• Press the **Home** key to get a better view of the spreadsheet.

——— **6.5 The @IF function** ———

You will now set up a section of the spreadsheet which will calculate the profit or loss of each share dealing and determine whether a gain is long- or short-term. So you are sure that you appreciate the nature of this problem, an explanation of the assumptions will first need to be stated.

The calculation of a profit or loss is to be based on the difference between the final purchase price for each set of shares and the final selling price. It needs to be borne in mind that not all shares are sold off; hence it is not simply a formula of amount less cost.

The criterion for short- or long-term gain will be whether the difference in the dates exceeds one year (365 days). If the dates are more than a year apart, then the gain or loss is long term, otherwise it is short term.

• Type in the following labels:

F14   Gain (Loss)
G14   Term.

Cell F16 is going to contain the degree of gain or loss. Think carefully about how this is worked out. You will need to get Lotus 1-2-3 to calculate how much you would have paid for the shares sold before you can determine the gain or loss. This will be the purchase price for the shares plus the commission, i.e. price shares sold for, less price paid for shares. Price shares sold for is the share selling price per share (cell C16) multiplied by the number sold (cell B16) *less* the commission. Price paid for shares is share purchase price per share (cell C8) multiplied by number sold (cell B16) *plus* the commission.

Think carefully about this before accepting the formula.

The formula is, therefore:

+B16*C16*(100%-$F$3) - C8*B16*(100%+$F$3)

- Type this formula into cell F16.
- Format the cell to currency and to 2 decimal places.
- Copy the formula and cell format in cell F16 to cells F17 to F18.

Now for the IF command that will determine whether the transaction is long term or short term. The logic of it goes something like this:

If the difference between the selling date and purchase date is greater than 365 then 'Long' will appear in cell G16. If not, 'Short' will appear.

To achieve this, click on cell G16 and type:

@IF(A16-A8>365,"Long","Short")

The @IF statement appears in brackets and is broken into three components.

The first part is the argument. In this case it was A16-A8>365, which calculates the value of cell A16 less the value of cell A8 (which are the dates in number format) and determines if it is greater than 365.

The second part appears after the first comma and is an instruction as to what should be done if the argument is true. In this instance, it is to place the word 'Long' in the cell.

The third part that appears after the second comma is an instruction as to what should be done if the argument is false. In this instance, it is to place the word 'Short' in the cell.

- Copy this formula from cell G16 to cells G17 to G18.
- Examine **Screen dump 6.5** to give you an idea of what you should have achieved by now.

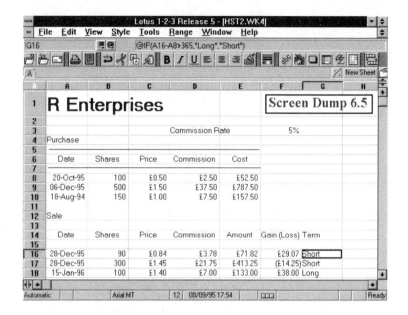

The last two entries made into your spreadsheet are complex, and you may need time to ponder over them. Experiment for a while by:

Altering the commission rate

Altering the dates

Altering the purchase and selling price of the shares.

- Save your spreadsheet as HST2 before moving on to the next section.
- Print out your spreadsheet, remembering to define the range to be printed.
- Click on File, then Close to put away your spreadsheet in preparation for the next one.

— 6.6 Relative and absolute formulae —

The next example uses a list of dates and numbers of caravans sold by a particular dealer over a particular year. See **Screen dump 6.6**. The example will give you further practice with developing formulae and achieving good presentation.

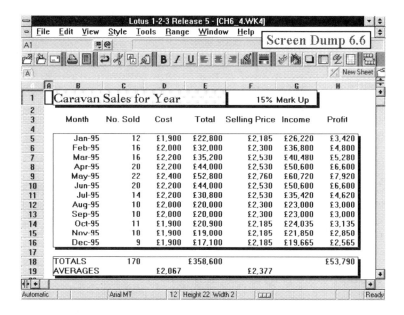

Screen Dump 6.6

Each month a number of caravans are sold (e.g. 10 in August). They cost £2,000 each, which is a total cost of £20,000. The 15% mark-up gives a selling price of £2,300 per caravan. The profit is worked out as the difference between selling price and cost price multiplied by the number sold.

- Type the title Caravan Sales for Year into cell A1, then change (to taste) Font & Attributes (click on Style, then Font & Attributes).
- Highlight cells A1 to C1, then give the range some lines, borders and colours in order to make the appearance more attractive (click on Style then Lines & Color).
- The column headings with cell locations are:

Cell	Label
A3	Month
B3	No. Sold
C3	Cost
D3	Total
E3	Selling Price
F3	Income
G3	Profit

- Widen column E so that the label Selling Price fits.
- Centre align the column headings (highlight cells A3 to G3, then click on the Centre align SmartIcon).
- Type in all the numbers sold in column B for the range of cells B5 to B16.
- Highlight cells B5 to B16.
- Click on Range, then Name, and type in SOLD, then click on the **OK** button.
- In cell F1 type in the label Mark Up.
- In cell E1 type 15%. If necessary format this cell using to Percent, to zero decimal places.

Next you will type in a date into cell A5 and get the program to calculate the remaining months. In order to appreciate the usefulness of this facility, it is wise to format the cells where the dates are to be typed in before putting dates into them.

- Highlight cells A5 to A16.
- Click on the left mouse button, ensuring the pointer is over the highlighted range. From the menu that appears, click on Number Format.
- Click on Date format and choose Dec-93. Click on the **OK** button. The cells will remain empty, but they have been formatted to all dates in the same way.
- In cell A5 type in the date using the @DATE function: @DATE(95,1,1).
- Now click on cell A6 and type in the formula +A5+31.

The purpose of this is to add 31 days to 1 January to go into February.

- Now copy the formula cell A6 to the range A7 to A16.

Each consecutive month should appear from January to December. Each cell containing this formula is derived by being 31 higher than the cell above. (It does not matter that the exact number of days for each month is not used.)

- At this stage, browse through the cells and examine each formula in the range A5 to A16 and be clear in your own mind about what has happened.

The concept of such formulae copying always taking a relative set of values is an important one. Look again to see how the concept works.

- Type the Cost figures in column C, using **Screen dump 6.6** to guide you.
- Click on cell D5 and type in a formula that will calculate the total cost of the caravans to the trader: +C5*B5.
- Now copy the formula in cell D5 to the destination range D6 to D16.

Again, observe what has happened in the cells in this range. Each formula is a multiple of the cell two positions to the left and one to the left.

Now you will see where this principle is not what is wanted in determining the selling price. The formula you want in cell E5 is one that multiplies the cost in cell C5 by the percentage mark-up set up in cell E1 added to the original cost. In fact, the formula will be: +(C5*E1)+C5. Note that the use of brackets ensures the multiplication is done before adding the original figure.

- Click on cell E5 and type in this formula.
- Now use the copy command to copy the formula in cell E5 to the destination range E6 through to E16.

Something has gone wrong!

Observe the formula in this range of cells and you will see that the percentage to work with is always assumed to be four cells directly above. In fact, although this relative position has worked in your favour up until now, you want to fix the cell E1 in the formula. Define an absolute cell value by placing a $ (dollar) sign in front of the cell location; in other words, instead of placing E1 in the formula, place $E$1.

- Click on cell E5 and amend the formula to: +(C5*$E$1)+C5.
- Now copy the formula in cell E5 to the destination range E7 to E16.

You should now have the desired result.

On a technical note, only the second part (the row number) needed to be fixed, as the column E bit would have stayed correct. Lotus 1-2-3 allows you to mix the absolute with relative references in a formula. In other words E$1 would have worked as well, making the formula +(C5*E$1)+C5.

- Click on cell F5 and type in the formula (E5*B5), then copy this formula to the range F6 to F16. This multiplies the selling price by the number sold to give the total income.

- To complete the spreadsheet, click on cell G5 and type in the formula +F5-D5, and then copy this formula to the range G6 to G16. This subtracts total cost from total income to give the profit.
- Highlight and Name the range G5 to G16 as PROFIT.
- Click cell A18 and type in label TOTAL.
- Click on cell B18 and type in the function @SUM(SOLD).
- Click on cell D18 and type in the function @SUM(COSTS).
- Click on cell G18 and type in the function @SUM(PROFIT).
- Click on cell A20 and type in the label AVERAGES.
- Highlight and Name the range C5 to C16 as COST.
- Click on cell A19 and type in the label AVERAGES.
- Click on cell C19 and type in the function @AVG(COST).
- Highlight and Name range E5 to E16 as SELLING.
- Click on cell E19 and type in the function @AVG(SELLING).

In order to tidy up your spreadsheet, do the following:

- Remove the grid lines (click on View, the Set View Preferences, then click on Grid Lines, then **OK**.
- Format all money figures to currency, with zero decimal places.
- Right align the cells A5 to A16.
- Highlight cells A5 to G16, and give them a border.
- Give a border and colour for the ranges: E1 to F1; A18 to G19.
- The spreadsheet is tighter against the left edge than it needs to be, so move it one column to the right by inserting a new column at Column A. Then alter the Column Width of column A to 3 characters.
- Save your spreadsheet for possible future reference and practice.

——— **6.7 Chapter summary** ———

As a brief concluding challenge to this chapter, try this problem:

Allow cell F18 (Total profit) to be typed in by the user. From this, the spreadsheet should determine the percentage mark up that is needed to get this profit and will then state the price that should be charged for the caravans each month.

In this chapter you have:

- manipulated text around the spreadsheet.
- formatted ranges with dates and currencies.

- typed in dates and further manipulated them using the @DATE function.
- copied relative and absolute formulae.
- had more practice on the presentation facilities with Lotus 1-2-3.
- used the @IF function to make decisions.
- moved ranges around a spreadsheet by either cut and paste or dragging a range to a new location.
- had more practice using named ranges to build formulae.

7

LOTUS 1-2-3
DATABASE

7.1 Aims of this chapter

This chapter examines the way Lotus 1-2-3 allows you to set up tables of data and then rearrange them into a different logical order. In doing so, it also examines a method whereby a table can be rearranged by a single operation from the keyboard rather than performing a whole string of command entries through Lotus 1-2-3 menus.

It is often useful to be able to extract certain information from a data table in, for example, unsold houses in a list of property details held by an estate agent. This example is developed in the latter part of this chapter.

7.2 Setting out a database table

Screen dump 7.1 shows you what you are trying to achieve in this chapter.

Here you will learn how to set up the program to rearrange the information: Surname, Date of Birth, Salary in ascending or descending order.

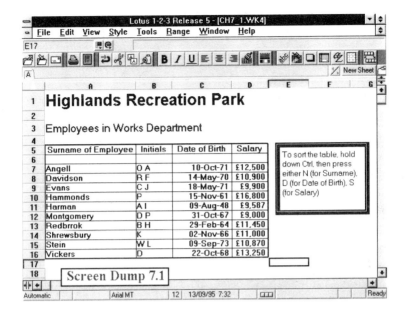

Screen Dump 7.1

When lists are exceptionally long, this facility is extremely useful. Also, if a single employee has to be added to the list, then you need only insert a new line on the spreadsheet, type in the details and use the **Ctrl** key command to rearrange the information back into sorted order. Before starting it is worth making yourself familiar with some of the jargon that this chapter will introduce you to.

A database can be defined as a collection of pieces of information organised in a meaningful way. Consider a phone directory, which lists names, addresses, and phone numbers. Each entry in the phone book is thus divided into three parts: name, address, phone number. In technical terms, each entry in the phone book is called a 'record'; each section into which each record is divided is called a 'field'. Once you have grasped these concepts, you are well on your way to understanding what databases are all about.

—— 7.3 Typing in record details ——

- Start by typing in the required header labels:

Cell	Label
A1	Highland Recreation Park
A3	Employees in Works Department
A5	Surname of Employee
B5	Initials
C5	Date of Birth
D5	Salary

- At this point you will need to widen columns A and C so that the labels can be seen.
- Give the title in cell A1 a more prominent appearance.

Next you will need to type in the details of each individual employee. Each row (or line) on the spreadsheet represents a record of an employee with the cell locations holding the fields Surname, Initials, Date of Birth and Salary.

- Type in the record details from **Screen dump 7.1**, remembering that dates will have to be typed in function form @DATE (year, month, day). Then you will have to format the date (Style, Number Format, Date, 30-Dec-93).
- Format the salary figures to Currency and to zero decimal places.

You will now add a text object on the spreadsheet. This text object will 'float' on the spreadsheet in the same way as a chart. Wherever such an object is placed, it will not cause any loss of data in the spreadsheet cells.

- Click on Tools, then Draw, then Text.
- Position the dotted cross that appears on cell E3 and click your mouse button. The floating text object will now appear, ready for you to type in the text.

Type in the following text, remembering *not* to press the **Enter** key:

To sort the table, hold down **Ctrl**, then press either N (for Surname), D (for Date of Birth), S (for Salary).

- Place the mouse pointer over the object, move the pointer to the edge and resize your text object for a best fit.

- Left click your mouse button over the text object and, from the menu that appears, add some lines and colour to give the object a more interesting appearance.

In your database you must ensure that:

1 The column contains one **field**.
2 Each field name is unique, i.e. does not appear twice.
3 Each **record** is kept on one row.

—— 7.4 Sorting the records ——

Before beginning with the sort, you should NAME certain parts of your spreadsheet in order to conform to better spreadsheet practice and get a better 'feel' for the concept of a database.

- Highlight cells A7 to D16. Left click your mouse button over the range and, using the small menu that appears, give the range the name DATABASE.
- Now repeat this for each field range, column by column.

Range	Name
A7 to A16	SURNAME
B7 to B16	INITIALS
C7 to C16	DATE OF BIRTH
D7 to D16	SALARY

The next task is to rearrange the records into Salary order.

- Click on <u>R</u>ange, then <u>S</u>ort.

Now you need to define the database range and how you want it sorted.

- In the <u>R</u>ange box, in the Sort dialogue box, type: DATABASE.

Having defined where the database range is, the next stage is to indicate what field you want the database sorted by.

- In the <u>S</u>ort by box, in the Sort dialogue box, type SALARY.
- The default setting should be <u>A</u>scending (determining how the records are sorted).
- Click on the Add <u>K</u>ey button.

In the event that you have more than one identical salary, you can then undergo a secondary sort by surname.

- In the Sort by box type SURNAME.

At this stage, the sort criterion has been set to that shown in **Screen dump 7.2**. Refer to this to make sure you have made your settings correct.

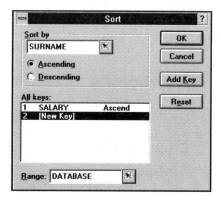

Screen Dump 7.2

- Now click on the **OK** button to see the effect.

Experiment by changing some of the salaries so that they are no longer in numerical order, and repeat the process.

It is important to note that data ranges can be sorted without having to name ranges in the way you have done throughout this chapter. If you have not named any ranges, then you would need to type in range co-ordinates rather than range names.

7.5 Sorting using macros

In many circumstances, you want to replace a sequence of commands with just one key stroke.

You will record the sorting procedure in a format called a macro. A macro simply performs a number of keystrokes for you. You will start the macro with the press of one key (or, in this case, holding down the **Ctrl** key and pressing one other key).

- Click on Tools, then Macro, then Record.

Everything you now do will be recorded until you tell the computer to stop recording. You will, therefore, proceed by carrying out a sorting procedure on your database so that the instructions are recorded.

- Click on Range, then Sort.
- In the Range box, in the Sort dialogue box, type: DATABASE.
- In the Sort by box, in the Sort dialogue box, type: SURNAME.
- The default setting should be Ascending.
- Click on the Add Key button.
- In the Sort by box type: INITIALS.
- Click on the **OK** button to see the database rearranged with surnames appearing in alphabetic order.

To stop the recording:

- Click on Tools, then Macro, then Stop Recording.
- Click again on Tools, then Macro, then Show Transcript.

A Transcript window will appear in the lower left-hand corner of the screen. This a transcript of what you have just done, and will vary a little according to what version of Lotus 1-2-3 you are using. See **Screen dump 7.3**.

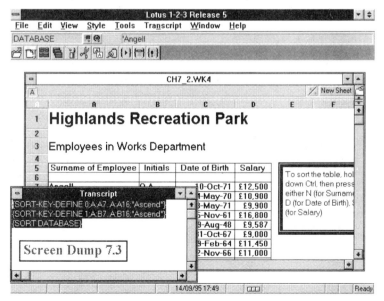

Screen Dump 7.3

In this Screen dump, the transcript text has been highlighted. You will also observe that a new set of SmartIcons will have appeared.

As you perform your commands, the Lotus 1-2-3 program is creating the sequence of commands that it uses to perform the actions. By recording commands in this way, you are effectively getting Lotus 1-2-3 to write a program for you. This will form the basis of your macro.

- With your mouse, highlight all the text that appears in the transcript window. You can increase the size of the transcript window by either dragging the right edge further right or clicking on the maximise button in the transcript window.
- Click on the Cut SmartIcon to store the macro in the Clipboard *and* to remove the text from the transcript window.
- Click back in the spreadsheet to cause the transcript window to disappear. Alternatively, you can click on the top left of the transcript window and click on Close.
- Click on cell A18 and then click on the Paste SmartIcon.

The contents of the transcript window will now be pasted to the spreadsheet, enabling you to assign a macro. The range A18 to A22 will now be named as the macro.

- Highlight cells A18 to A22
- Click on Range, then Name and, in the Name box in the Name dialogue box, type in \N.
- Click on the OK button.
- Alter the Surname Davidson to Williams.
- Hold down the **Ctrl** key and press the N key on your keyboard; the records will now sort into surname order, and then initial order where two surnames are the same.
- Repeat these instructions for Date of Birth (\D) and Salary (\S). When you get to the Sort dialogue box, you will need to click on Reset before you type in the new sorting criterion.

The respective transcripts are shown in **Screen dump 7.4**. The actual transcripts that your version of Lotus 1-2-3 creates may differ from the one that appears in this Screen dump.

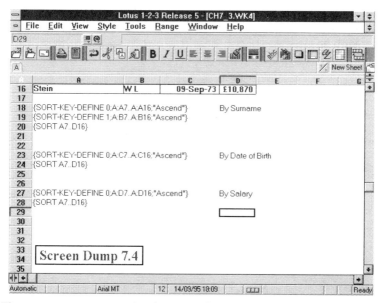

The macros *must* stay in the spreadsheet. They can, however, be moved well out of the way by highlighting the range where they have been pasted and dragging them elsewhere on the spreadsheet.

● Alter some of the names, dates of birth and salaries and experiment with the macros.

7.6 Macro buttons

As well as being able to assign a macro to a key stroke, you can also create a macro button on the screen which, when clicked on, carries out the function. This will be done as an alternative to using the **Ctrl** key and is much easier for a user to follow.

● Click on the text floating object that contains the instructions on how to activate the macros.
● Click on the **Delete** key on your keyboard to remove the object.

- Click on Tools, then Draw, then Button. The pointer becomes a black cross. Hold down the left mouse button and drag the cross to form an elongated button where the text object used to be. Let go of the mouse button.

Screen Dump 7.5

Screen dump 7.5 shows the Assign to Button dialogue box which requires you to assign a macro to the button and what text you want to appear on the button.

- In the Assign to Button dialogue box, click on the arrow in the Assign macro from: box, and click on Range.
- Highlighlight the Range box and select the range name \S from the list of range names in the Existing named ranges box.
- Highlight the Button text box and type in the label Sort by Surname.
- Click on the **OK** button.
- Now drag the button to where you want it on the spreadsheet.

Clicking on the new button performs the macro. If you click on the button with the right mouse button, you can resize the button, drag it to another location, change the label, and its fonts, etc.

- Now create macro buttons for the other two sort macros.

Screen dump 7.6 shows what you should finally have. Before moving on to the next section, save your spreadsheet and experiment with your buttons.

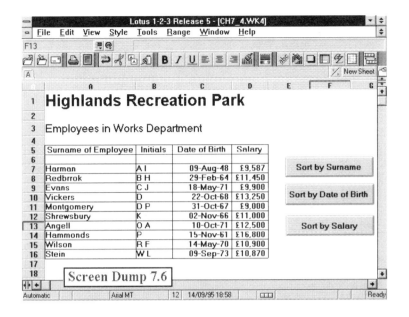

Highlands Recreation Park

Employees in Works Department

Surname of Employee	Initials	Date of Birth	Salary
Harman	A I	09-Aug-48	£9,587
Redbrrok	B H	29-Feb-64	£11,450
Evans	C J	18-May-71	£9,900
Vickers	D	22-Oct-68	£13,250
Montgomery	D P	31-Oct-67	£9,000
Shrewsbury	K	02-Nov-66	£11,000
Angell	O A	10-Oct-71	£12,500
Hammonds	P	15-Nov-61	£16,800
Wilson	R F	14-May-70	£10,900
Stein	W L	09-Sep-73	£10,870

Sort by Surname

Sort by Date of Birth

Sort by Salary

Screen Dump 7.6

7.7 Extracting information from a database

In this part of the chapter, you will use the Data Query part of the program to extract certain specified items from a list. Examine **Screen dump 7.7**.

The aim is quite simple: to extract from the table a list of all those houses that have not been sold. Start by acquainting yourself with some more jargon. What you do is set up a query table on to which you will copy all the required data. The criterion section will represent the table from which you want to select the data.

• Begin by typing in all the details on a new spreadsheet. You will need to widen some columns to fit the labels.

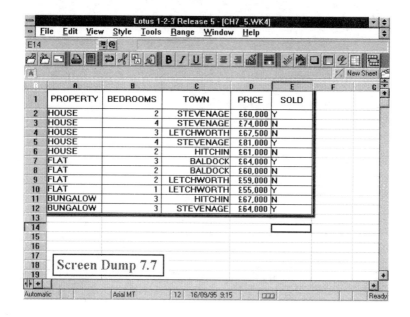

	PROPERTY	BEDROOMS	TOWN	PRICE	SOLD
1	PROPERTY	BEDROOMS	TOWN	PRICE	SOLD
2	HOUSE	2	STEVENAGE	£60,000	Y
3	HOUSE	4	STEVENAGE	£74,000	N
4	HOUSE	3	LETCHWORTH	£67,500	N
5	HOUSE	4	STEVENAGE	£81,000	Y
6	HOUSE	2	HITCHIN	£61,000	N
7	FLAT	3	BALDOCK	£64,000	Y
8	FLAT	2	BALDOCK	£60,000	N
9	FLAT	2	LETCHWORTH	£59,000	N
10	FLAT	1	LETCHWORTH	£55,000	Y
11	BUNGALOW	3	HITCHIN	£67,000	N
12	BUNGALOW	3	STEVENAGE	£64,000	Y

Screen Dump 7.7

In **Screen dump 7.7** the Alignment option from the Style pull-down menu was used to justify the town names in Column C to the right of their cells. Also, the prices are displayed in £s. The table has also been given a frame.

At this stage the database is the range from cell A1 to cell E12. Each row (house details) represents a single record in the database, while each cell in a row represents a field. You have 11 records from row 2 to row 12, and each record has five fields; column A to column E. This is a simple principle well worth getting used to. At the top of each column is the field name, which will have an important part to play in the demonstration.

- Highlight cells A1 to E12.
- Click on <u>T</u>ools, then <u>D</u>atabase, then <u>N</u>ew Query.

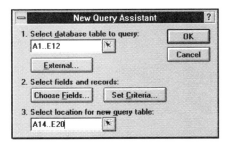

Screen Dump 7.8

Screen dump 7.8 shows the resulting dialogue box with the various settings for the Database Table and the Location for a new Query Table. The database table range comprises the cells where the computer is going to look for the records. Here it is the range A1 to E12. It is important to note that the database table *must* include the field names at the top of each column. This is different from the Database Range used earlier in this chapter to sort data, which excluded the field names.

- At this point, box 1 should show the database table as A1..E12. If not, then enter this into box 1.
- Click on box 3: select a location for the new query table.
- Type in A14..E20, which is the location directly underneath the database table.

You can place the new query table anywhere on the spreadsheet, but if you position it underneath the database table, the column widths are already set up correctly to suit the data, although there is no absolute need for this.

The next stage is to enter details about a criterion. The program needs this to determine what you want selected from the database table. In this example, you will work on the basis of selecting details of all unsold houses. **Screen dump 7.9** shows the Set Criteria dialogue box where the records to be selected for the query table will be where the SOLD field is equal to N.

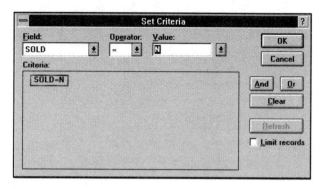

Screen Dump 7.9

- Click on the Set Criteria button in box 2 of the New Query Assistant dialogue box.
- In the Set Criteria dialogue box, click on the Field arrow button.

All the fields in the highlighted database will be listed: Property; Bedrooms; Town; Price; Sold.

- Click on SOLD.
- Move to the Value box and click on the arrow button. The fields Y and N will appear, click on N, then click on the **OK** button to return to the New Query Assistant dialogue box.

The criterion has now been set up so that where SOLD=N in the database table, the record will be copied to the query table. Now you will select all fields to appear in the query table except the SOLD field. **Screen dump 7.10** shows the Choose Fields dialogue box.

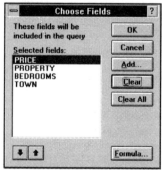

Screen Dump 7.10

- Click on the Choose Fields button from the New Query Assistant dialogue box.
- Click on the SOLD field name from the Selected field box and then click on the Clear button.
- Now click on the **OK** button to return to the New Query Assistant dialogue box.
- Now click on the **OK** button in this dialogue box and you will be returned to the spreadsheet.
- You should now have the results shown in **Screen dump 7.11**.

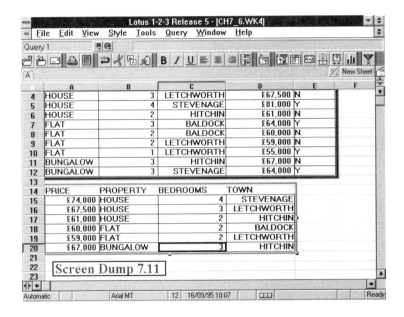

Screen Dump 7.11

Now try the following:

- Click on Tools, then Database, then New query.
- Set up the following parameters:

database table (box 1)	A1..E12
new query (box 3)	A22..E33
set Criterion	Price > £64,000

The top section of **Screen dump 7.12** shows how the above criterion needs to be set. When you activate this, you will see, in the new query range, an extract of all properties with a price greater than £64,000.

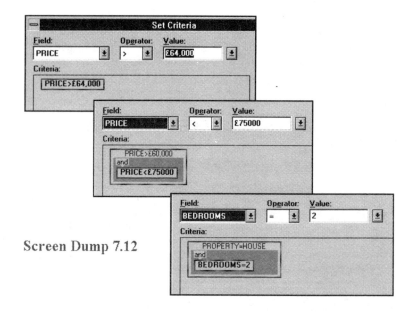

Screen Dump 7.12

- Click on Tools, then Database, then New query.
- Set up the following parameters:

  database table (box 1)   A1..E12
  new query (box 3)   A28..E33
  set Criteria   Price > £60,000
                                AND
                                Price < £75,000

- You will need to set two lines of criteria. When you have set the first one, click on the And button to set the second.

The middle section of **Screen dump 7.12** shows how the above criterion needs to be set. When you activate this, you will see, in the new query range, an extract of all properties with a price greater than £60,000 and less than £75,000.

- Click on Tools, then Database, then New query.

• Set up the following parameters:

database table (box 1)   A1..E12
new query (box 3)   A35..E44

set Criteria   Property = HOUSE
                         AND
                         Bedrooms = 2

The bottom section of **Screen dump 7.12** shows how the above criterion needs to be set. When you activate this, you will see, in the new query range, an extract of all properties listed as a house and with 2 bedrooms.

In practice, such databases may run into many hundreds of records and such facilities can prove very useful. It should also be noted that the query table can be placed on to another sheet rather than below a database table on an existing sheet. Once you have grasped the basics of performing such query analysis, setting up more sophisticated spreadsheets will not prove such a difficult step.

The final part of this section looks at deleting and finding various records in a database. Before going any further, it would be wise to save your spreadsheet in case you ever want to refer back to it. Before deleting records, it is often a good idea to save the current version of the spreadsheet in case the deleted records are needed again.

• Click on Tools, then Database, then Delete Records.

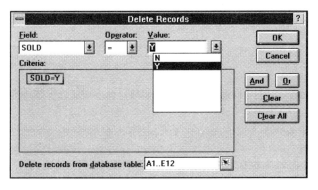

Screen Dump 7.13

If you observe **Screen dump 7.13** you will see the Delete Records dialogue box. Again, the database table has to be defined as A1..E12. Other boxes require criteria in the same way as you used before. In this example the criterion will have been set so that the field where SOLD=Y will be deleted.

- Type in the database table range and the criterion as in **Screen dump 7.13**.
- Click on the **OK** button to see the results.

If you wish to restore the deleted records at this stage, you can click on the UNDO SmartIcon to reverse the action.

- Click on the Undo SmartIcon in order to work on the next activity. If this does not work, then restore the spreadsheet you saved prior to deleting records.

The Find Records options in the Tools, Database menu works in exactly the same way as the Delete Records, except nothing is deleted – the records that meet the criteria in the database table are all highlighted.

- Click on Tools, then Database, then Find Records.
- Define the database table as A1..E12 and then set the criteria as:

Field	Operator	Value
Town	=	Stevenage
AND		
Property	=	House

- Click on the **OK** button.

Three records in the database will be highlighted.

− 7.8 Further work with a database −

In this third example you will attempt to set up a simple database of stock records, from it sort the records into value or stock reference order and print a list using a macro.

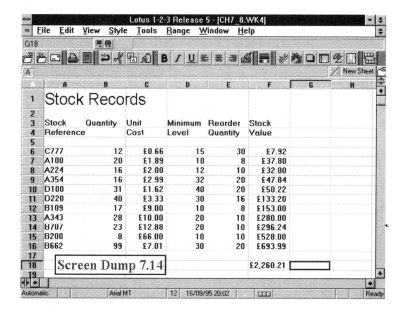

To get yourself started examine **Screen dump 7.14** to see what kind of layout is required and the cell entries you want, observing the following points before typing in values, formulae and formats:

- The field Stock Reference contains labels.
- The fields Quantity, Unit Cost, Minimum Level, and Reorder Quantity are numeric entries.
- The Stock Value field contains formulae entries: Quantity multiplied by Unit Cost (both formatted for currency to 2 decimal places).
- Cell F18 is a @SUM function summing all Stock Values.
- The following ranges are NAMED (Click on Range, then Name).

Range	Name
A6..F16	Stock data
A6..A16	Stock Reference
B6..B16	Quantity
C6..C16	Unit Cost
D6..D16	Minimum Level
E6..E16	Reorder Quantity
F6..F16	Stock Value

— 7.9 Tracing commands for macros —

In this final section you will write a macro to sort the table by value and then for yourself, do the same for reference.

- Click on Tools, then Macro, then Record.
- Click on Range, then Sort.
- In the Sort dialogue box, click on the Range box and type in the range name: STOCK DATA.
- In the Sort by box, type in the range name STOCK VALUE, click on Descending, then click on the **OK** button.

The database range will be highlighted and reordered according to Stock Value, with the highest value in the top line.

- Click on Tools, then Macro, then Stop Recording.
- Click on Tools, then Macro, then Show Transcript to reveal the transcript window over the spreadsheet, as shown in **Screen dump 7.15**.

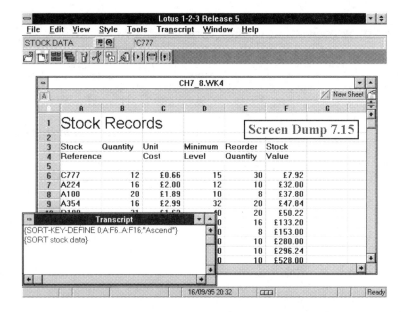

- Highlight the entire transcript and copy it to the Clipboard by clicking on the Copy SmartIcon.
- Move the pointer to the spreadsheet, click on the spreadsheet and move to cell A20.
- Click on the Paste SmartIcon to paste the transcript to the spreadsheet.
- Highlight cells A22 to A25, left click your mouse with the pointer over the range, and name the range \S.

Now, if you hold down the **Ctrl** key and press S, the macro will reorder the table into descending order based on Stock Value.

- Click on the Quantity column to change some of the values and see if it works.
- Now create a button to perform this, as you did with the Highlands Recreation Park table.

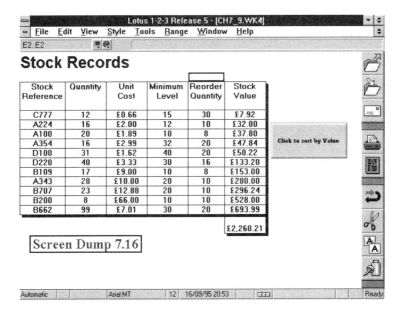

Stock Records

Stock Reference	Quantity	Unit Cost	Minimum Level	Reorder Quantity	Stock Value
C777	12	£0.66	15	30	£7.92
A224	16	£2.00	12	10	£32.00
A100	20	£1.89	10	8	£37.80
A354	16	£2.99	32	20	£47.84
D100	31	£1.62	40	20	£50.22
D220	40	£3.33	30	16	£133.20
B109	17	£9.00	10	8	£153.00
A343	28	£10.00	20	10	£280.00
B707	23	£12.88	20	10	£296.24
B200	8	£66.00	10	10	£528.00
B662	99	£7.01	30	20	£693.99

£2,260.21

Click to sort by Value

Screen Dump 7.16

Screen dump 7.16 shows the final results with a few alterations to the appearance to make it look more interesting.

- Use the View, Set View Preferences to remove some of the spread-sheet features.
- Use Tools, SmartIcons, Position to alter the position of the SmartIcons and use Tools, SmartIcons, Icon size to alter their size.
- Finally, create a macro and assign it to a button that will sort the database table into reference order.

———— 7.10 Chapter summary ————

This chapter has covered many aspects of database activity although a good deal has been left out. The activities that have been left out are the more advanced features of the database utilities and are beyond the scope of a book like this, which has been written as an introduction to the package.

In this chapter, you have:

- defined the term database.
- entered a structured database with records on rows and field titles at the top of columns.
- sorted records into logical sequence.
- written a macro by tracing the sequence of commands into a transcript window and then copied them to the spreadsheet.
- created buttons and assigned macros to them.
- set up a query and extract data from a defined database table into a query table, using given criteria.
- located a record from a database range, using given criteria.
- deleted records from a database table, using given criteria.

8

MORE ON GRAPHS AND CHARTS

8.1 Aims of this chapter

This chapter aims to give you the opportunity to develop your knowledge and skills with the Lotus graphs and charts beyond that used in Chapters 4 and 5. Lotus 1-2-3 offers a wide range of facilities in charts, each with varying types and presentation. There is also an annotation facility which allows you to enhance your charts further. Release 5 and above users have the added facility of being able to create maps and to label regions, states and countries on the map.

At this stage in the book it is assumed that the reader knows how to set up a spreadsheet and produce a basic chart. If you have forgotten any points, refer to previous chapters.

8.2 More on bar charts

This section examines bar charts using a different example from those previously used and allows you to show data in different perspectives. **Screen dump 8.1** shows a spreadsheet of an insurance company's premiums over a given year.

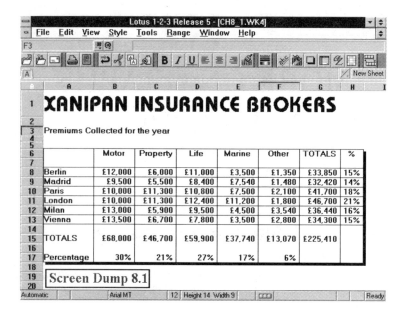

XANIPAN INSURANCE BROKERS

Premiums Collected for the year

	Motor	Property	Life	Marine	Other	TOTALS	%
Berlin	£12,000	£6,000	£11,000	£3,500	£1,350	£33,850	15%
Madrid	£9,500	£5,500	£8,400	£7,540	£1,480	£32,420	14%
Paris	£10,000	£11,300	£10,800	£7,500	£2,100	£41,700	18%
London	£10,000	£11,300	£12,400	£11,200	£1,800	£46,700	21%
Milan	£13,000	£5,900	£9,500	£4,500	£3,540	£36,440	16%
Vienna	£13,500	£6,700	£7,800	£3,500	£2,800	£34,300	15%
TOTALS	£68,000	£46,700	£59,900	£37,740	£13,070	£225,410	
Percentage	30%	21%	27%	17%	6%		

Screen Dump 8.1

Remember you cannot simply copy the figures in the spreadsheet. Note the following with regard to the data:

- Totals are established using the @SUM function.
- The percentages are derived using a formula. The formula in cell H8 is +G8/$G$15) (i.e. the total for Berlin expressed as a percentage of the grand total).

The dollar sign in the formula sets an absolute cell reference. This was discussed at length in Chapter 6.

- The values that appear in the cells are then formatted to percent, to zero decimal places.

Once you have typed in the spreadsheet, you can work on the charts.

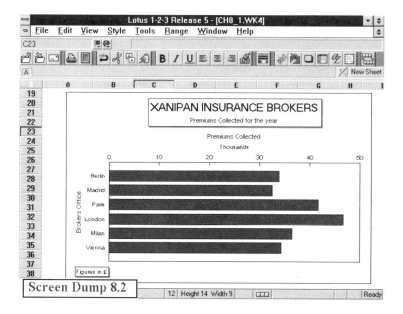

Screen Dump 8.2

The chart in **Screen dump 8.2** is no different in construction from the one set up in Chapter 4, except that it is not three dimensional and it has been rotated. However, it will prove a useful starting point. You will use the following procedure for preparing a chart:

1 Prepare the initial data in the spreadsheet with a set of appropriately named ranges.

2 Decide where on the spreadsheet the chart is to go, remembering that charts are floating objects and, although they can obscure parts of your spreadsheets, they cannot overwrite data on a spreadsheet.

3 Identify the X variable (what you want to measure the numbers against). With the chart in **Screen dump 8.2**, the premiums collected are shown against Broker's Office. Consequently, Broker's Office has become the X variable.

4 Determine the Y variable(s). The chart in Screen dump 8.2 has the total premiums collected by that particular office set as the Y Axis.

5 Give the chart titles and labels to make it easy for a user to see what it is showing.

With all these stages in mind, you can now reproduce the chart shown in **Screen dump 8.2**, assuming that at this stage you have prepared your spreadsheet on the basis of that show in **Screen dump 8.1**.

- Click on Range, then Name.

- Click on the Range box in the Name dialogue and name the following cell ranges using the following technique: Click on the Range box, then click on the button with the left pointing arrow at the end of the Range box. The dialogue box will temporarily disappear, allowing you to highlight where the cells are you want to name. When you take your finger off the mouse button, having highlighted the cells, the range will be automatically written in the Range box, allowing you to click on the Name box and type in the range name. Click on the Add button and repeat.

Name	Range
TYPES	B6..F6
TOTAL TYPE	B15..F15
TOTAL OFFICE	G8..G13
MOTOR	B8..B13
PROPERTY	C8..C13
LIFE	D8..D13
MARINE	E8..E13
OTHER	F8..F13
BERLIN	B8..F8
MADRID	B9..F9
PARIS	B10..F10
LONDON	B11..F11
MILAN	B12..F12
VIENNA	B13..F13

This method of naming ranges is designed to conform to good spreadsheet practice by making the setting up of the charts easier to follow, as you will soon appreciate.

- Move the cell pointer to a clear area of your spreadsheet so that you can place a chart over the spreadsheet without obscuring the data you typed in.
- Click on Tools, then Chart. If you are a Release 5 user, then a dialogue box will appear requiring a data range, just click on the **OK** button.

- Now size the chart, with your mouse, to fill the screen, then click on the Bar chart SmartIcon.
- Click on Chart, then Ranges.
- Click on X-axis labels in the Series box of the Ranges dialogue box. In the Range box, type: LOCATION. Then click on the A-data in the Series box. Click again on the Range box, and type: TOTAL OFFICE. Then click on the **OK** button.

At this stage you have a single Y variable which is defined as the A series with the data contained in the named range TOTAL OFFICE. You should now give the chart a title.

- Double click on the Title box that appears on your chart.

Instead of typing in a title, Lotus 1-2-3 allows you to specify a label that already appears on the spreadsheet. In this case, cell A1 contains the main title and cell A3 a sub-title. Observe **Screen dump 8.3** and you will see how you can set up the headings in the Headings dialogue box to take advantage of this.

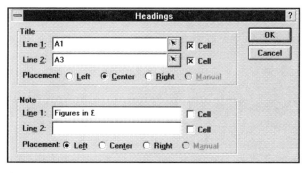

Screen Dump 8.3

- On Line 1: of the Title box, enter A1 in the box and then click on the Cell box to its right.
- On Line 2: of the Title box, enter A3 in the box and then click on the Cell box to its right.
- On Line 1: of the Note box, enter the text Figures in £ in the box. With the placement set as Left, the text will then appear bottom left of the chart area.
- Now click on the **OK** button.

- Click on the Chart type SmartIcon (or click on Chart, then Type). Click on the Horizontal Orientation box, then click on the **OK** button.

You now have the basics of the chart. Next you must label the axis.

- Click on Chart, then Axis, then X-axis.
- Click on the Axis title box and type the title: Brokers Office. Then click on the **OK** button.
- Repeat this for the Y-axis typing the label: Premiums Collected. Then click on the **OK** button.
- Click on the Data A box that appears on your chart area, then press the **Delete** key on your keyboard. It will be deleted and allows the bar area to be expanded to fill more of the chart area.
- Now save your spreadsheet with name bars.

In the next section, you will delete this chart and create another.

———— 8.3 Multiple bar charts ————

The problem with the chart as it stands is that it fails to show all the information available in the spreadsheet. The totals show which brokers are the largest but the chart does not break down the size of the business in each category as shown in the spreadsheet.

Look at **Screen dump 8.4**. Instead of showing the totals for each office, this shows the size of each category for each office.

There are in fact few differences between the two charts beyond the stark appearances. The titles are still the same and the X-axis has not been altered. One problem that has been taken away from you is the size of the scale. If you observe the Y-axis you will see that the scale ranges from zero at the bottom to 15,000 at the top. In **Screen dump 8.2** the scale range was from zero to 50,000. Lotus works all this out for you.

Each City broker is represented by five bars, one for each category of insurance. The bar for each insurance category is explained to the right of the chart by the legends. This is an extra you ought to put on your chart if an observer is to understand what is being shown.

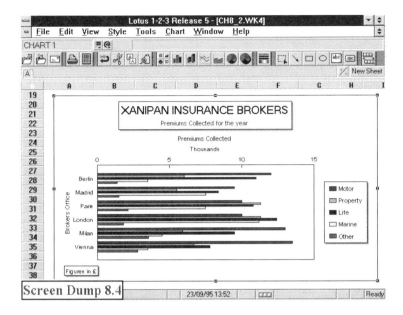

Screen Dump 8.4

First, delete the chart currently active:

- Click on the chart area near its edge and press the **Delete** key on your keyboard.
- Click on Tools, then Chart. If you are a Release 5 user, click on **OK** to the dialogue box that appears.
- Size up the chart to fill your screen.
- Click on the Chart Type SmartIcon, then click on Horizontal Orientation, then on the **OK** button.
- Double click on the Title box on your chart area and enter the cell locations of the headings as you did before: Line 1 at cell A1 and Line 2 at cell A3. Also type in Line 1 of the Note: Figures in £. Click on the **OK** button when done.
- Click on Chart, then Axis, and type in Brokers Office. Repeat this for the Y-axis with the title Premiums Collected.
- Click on Chart pull, then Ranges option and type in the following ranges:

Series	Range
X	LOCATION
A	MOTOR
B	PROPERTY
C	LIFE
D	MARINE
E	OTHER

All that now remains is to enter the legends needed to identify what each bar represents.

● Click on Chart, then Legends, and type in the following legends.

A	MOTOR
B	PROPERTY
C	LIFE
D	MARINE
E	OTHER.

● Now view the chart to see what you have achieved. Use the 3-D bar chart SmartIcon for a different look at your chart.

Because you used named ranges rather than cell locations to identify ranges, the entering of both series and legend titles became simple and quite logical.

8.4 Changing the perspectives of your chart

Begin by comparing your result with **Screen dump 8.5**.

You now have a chart that shows, for each office, the amount of premiums collected for each category of insurance. Suppose that you want to show, for each category of insurance, how much each office has collected. **Screen dump 8.5** shows an example of this.

In this instance the X-axis variable is the category of insurance while the Y-axis variables are the six city offices. You can now see the relative importance of each category of insurance more clearly and how much each office has contributed to the total.

To achieve this perspective of the data you need to alter X and Y variables as well as the legends. You will also have to change the title

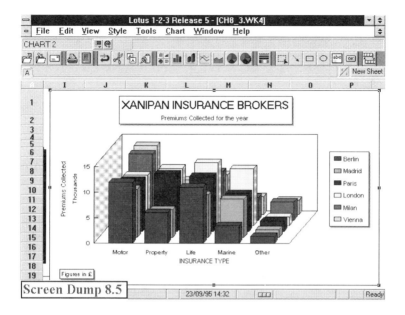

on the X-axis. The rest will be much the same as before.

• Below the chart already in existence, create another chart area to fill your screen.

• Click on Chart, then Headings and identify the cell of A1 as being the Line 1 title and cell A3 as Line 2 as you did previously. Type in Figures in £ as Note Line 1.

• Click on Chart, then Ranges, and name the ranges as follows:

   X   INSURANCE TYPE
   Y   Premiums Collected.

• Click on Chart, then Ranges, type in the variable ranges as follows:

Series	Range
X	TYPES
A	BERLIN
B	MADRID
C	PARIS
D	LONDON
E	MILAN
F	VIENNA.

• Now click on <u>C</u>hart, then Legend and type in the legends, as above.

Your chart should now show the desired result. The 3-D effect works better here because the X-axis titles are smaller. However, you may find some of the bars a little obscured. In the next section you will see a possible alternative to this.

——— 8.5 Stacked bar chart ———

Looking at **Screen dump 8.5** you may not be satisfied that the reader can tell at a glance the size of each category of insurance. Observe the stacked bar chart in **Screen dump 8.6** to see the data in a different way.

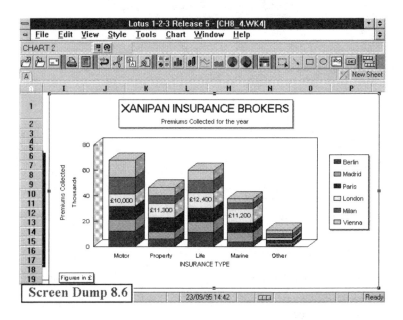

This chart uses one bar for each category on the X-axis while splitting up the bar into components for each of the Y variables. Again the scales have been drawn up for you.

• Click on the Chart Types SmartIcon, then the Stacked Bar Icon, then click on the **OK** button.

Everything has been done for you in terms of the scaling.

You can label particular parts of your chart. In this example, you will bring to attention the premiums collected by the London office.

- Click on Chart, then Data Labels.
- Highlight D in the Series box, click on Range of the labels box, type in London, and click on the **OK** button.

You can now see the effect for yourself. You could, of course, do this for all labels, but your chart might look too congested.

8.6 The pie chart with some annotation

In order to get a different view of the data, you can produce a pie chart that shows first the share of total premium contribution by the Office and then the share of total premium by their category. **Screen dump 8.7** shows both such charts.

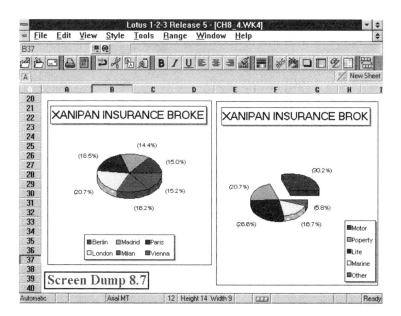

You can see at a glance the relative contribution each has made to the total. In the Pie Chart that shows Insurance by Type, the motor segment has been removed from the rest of the pie like a slice of cake being cut – a technique called 'exploding'. This can be extremely useful if you want to highlight one particular segment.

You will also notice in **Screen dump 8.8** that text has been added to it to indicate that London is a record high. This was created by the Annotate facility.

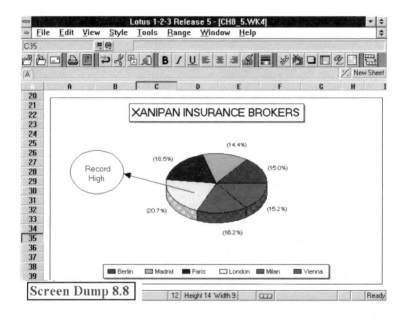

Screen Dump 8.8

In order to create a pie chart, a little less information is required than was needed for the bar charts. All you need is an X variable to determine what each portion of the pie represents and a variable to determine which figures to measure against, plus some titles at the top.

- Create a new chart as before, then click on the 3-D Pie Chart SmartIcon.
- Set Ranges as follows:

Series	Range
X	LOCATION
A (Slice label)	TOTAL OFFICE.

- Click on Chart, then Headings and create the two headings as before.
- Double click on the Legends box that appears on your chart, and enter the Legends for each of the cities in the same way as you did before. When this has been done, click on the option to place the legend below the chart and then click on the **OK** button.

If the figures are unclear, click on one of them. It will become surrounded by four black squares. Click on the right mouse button, then on Fonts & Attributes. Click on 12 in the Size box in the Fonts & Attributes dialogue box, then click on the **OK** button.

When adding annotated objects to a chart, you need to be aware that these too are floating objects, quite distinct from the chart itself. This means that if you alter the chart or its position, the annotated objects remain where they were originally placed. It is wise, therefore, to place such objects on to charts when you are certain about the size and final location of your chart.

- Click on Tools, then Draw, then Arrow.
- Now position the black cross in the pie segment for London (20.7%) and, keeping the mouse key depressed, drag a line from this segment. When you have a line of the required length, double click your mouse to see the arrow head appear.

This arrow now becomes an OBJECT. It can be moved if you feel you have made a mess. A single click over an object will cause small boxes to appear along it, indicating that the object is the subject of editing. If the object is the subject and you press your **Delete** key, it will disappear. In fact, while an object is the subject, you can carry out editing activities via the Edit pull down menu. By double clicking on the arrow you can produce a Lines & Color dialogue box and change its appearance.

- Now create a circle at the end of the arrow by clicking on the Circle icon (or Click on Tools, then Draw, then Circle) and then, use the mouse to control the size of the object, as you did with the arrow.

The text can be added in much the same way.

- Click on <u>T</u>ools, then <u>D</u>raw, then <u>T</u>ext and type in the words Record High, pressing the **Enter** or **Return** key between words.
- Now move the object with your mouse to its required location and double click.
- Reduce its size and move the object to its required location in the same way as you would any other object.

If an unwanted border appears, you can double click on the text to produce a Lines & Color dialogue box and indicate the border is to be None.

This can all take some dexterity and practice, but adding annotated objects to your chart allows a good many imaginative additions to be made. You will, however, have a problem when you resize and move your chart. The annotated objects will remain where they were originally created and stay the same size. Consequently, such objects will have to be moved along with the chart or created on the charts when you have decided on the permanent location of the chart.

This has completed the first pie chart. Now go on to create the next pie chart.

- Create another Chart in exactly the same as you did before, selecting a 3-D pie chart again.
- As before, identify the headings for the chart.
- Set range as:

Variable   Range

X   TYPES
A   TOTAL TYPE.

- Finally, to achieve what appears in **Screen dump 8.7**, try and resize and move both charts into a clear area of your spreadsheet and position them side by side. To create the explosion effect, click on the pie segment and, holding down the mouse button, move the slice away from the rest of the slices. You can also move the title box and legend box to wherever you want by clicking on the respective box, and moving it in the same way as you would move any other object.

At this stage save your work. The entire spreadsheet, when saved, will also hold all your charts. Hence, in a single operation, everything is saved.

Before going on to the next section, you are advised to practise calling up different charts, altering some of the numeric data on the spreadsheet to some of your own figures and viewing the differences that occur. Remember, you can position your charts next to the spreadsheet data, allowing you to see any changes made to the charts as you alter them. When you have finished experimenting with this, you will need to retrieve your present file in order to complete the chapter material.

8.7 Line graphs

In this next section you will go on to develop a different set of charts for which the data you already have is not really appropriate. By means of extension, you will set up an additional table of data showing the number of insurance claims made over the year as well as the amount paid out to those claiming. Examine **Screen dump 8.9** to see what you need to do to set up the initial data.

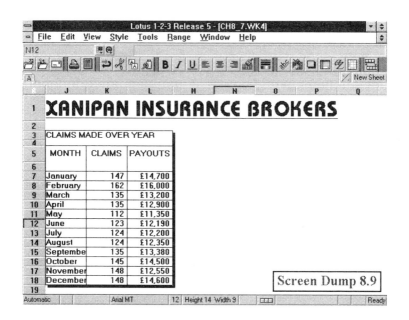

Screen Dump 8.9

The table has been placed to the right of the other table and shows two variables: number of claims and amount paid out, against one time variable.

- Press function key **F5**, type J1 in the second box, the click on the **OK** button.

You will now create the data exactly as it appears in **Screen dump 8.9** with the aid of a quick tip.

- Type in January in cell J7, then click on the large tick.
- Highlight cells J7 to J18 where the months are to go.
- Click on Range, then Fill by Example. The months will automatically be filled in.
- Enter the set of numbers that appear in columns K and L. Format the payouts to appear as currency and to zero decimal places.
- Make any alterations to the Style you feel appropriate. An exact likeness to **Screen dump 8.9** is not necessary for this exercise.
- As has now become normal practice, name three of the ranges that will be needed to set up the charts:

Range	Name
J7..J18	MONTH
K8..K18	CLAIMS
L8..L18	PAYOUTS.

- Draw a new chart as you have done before.
- Click on the Chart Type SmartIcon and click on 3-D Line.
- Of the charts available, click on the one where one line appears to cross the other, then click on the **OK** button.

The Plain Line option can be tried later.

You now need to determine the variables. As is normal, you want to see how things have changed over time, so use MONTH as the X-axis Series. In the first chart of this section, you will be looking at how the numbers of claims have changed over the year. As the A-data Series, use CLAIMS.

- Click on Chart, then Ranges and specify the two Series required.
- Give your chart the required headings and label the axes with the following titles:

X Title	MONTH
Y Title	NUMBER OF CLAIMS.

As with the bar charts, the scale has been worked out for you. You can see quite clearly how the number of claims made alters over the year.

You are now in a position to enter the amount in pounds claimed over the year and place these details on to the same chart. Doing this will simply mean adding another variable. It will alter the scales quite considerably and you will need to label the Y-axis to inform observers that it is used to measure both number of claims and amount in pounds.

- Click on Chart, then Ranges. Highlight B-data in the Series box, then type PAYOUTS in the Range box.
- Now take a look at the chart.

The problem should be an obvious one; you are unable to get a proper view of the number of claims because the Y-axis covers too wide a range; from just 112 to 16,000. You will need to reduce this range if you are to get a readable chart.

As a solution, you could express the amount claimed in hundreds. This would reduce the range of numbers from 112 to 160. This will mean, however, creating a new range of values to plot from on the spreadsheet. The method will involve creating a new column of figures and then hiding it from view.

- Go back to your spreadsheet and type into cell M7 the formula +L7/100 and copy this formula to the range M8 to M18.
- Click on Range, then Name.
- Click on PAYOUTS in the Existing named ranges and change the range to M7..M18.
- Now hide the newly created range. You can do this by clicking Style, then Format, then Hidden and type in the range name PAYOUTS, then click on the **OK** button.

You should now be able to see why it is useful to show amounts claimed in hundreds of £s against the number of claims. This chart now needs some alterations to improve its appearance.

- Click on Chart, then Axis, then Y-axis. Amend the Axis title to read: Number of Claims/£00s.
- Now click on Chart, then Legend. Type in new Legend entries:

    A   Number of Claims
    B   Amount Claimed.

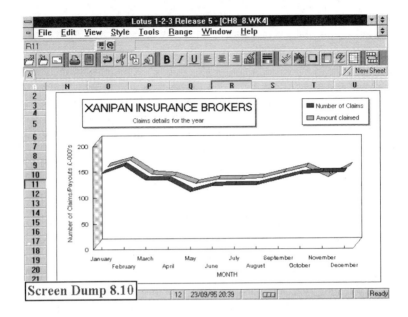

Screen Dump 8.10

The chart, as shown in **Screen dump 8.10** (yours will not be quite the same; see below) has a three-dimensional effect with two ribbon-like lines representing the two variables. The one in front (the A range) is the number of claims and the one behind (the B range), the amount claimed.

The title and legend boxes can now be moved. In **Screen dump 8.10**, the title box has been moved left, the legend box moved up. This is done by click and drag as with moving any other object. This has then meant more room to stretch the chart rightwards.

Before going into the next section, it is worth examining a method by which you can determine the scale on the axis rather than having it automatically set. By example, you will set the Y-axis to go from zero up to 100, an extension at both the upper and lower ends of the axis.

● Click on Chart then Axis, then Y-Axis.
● In the Scale manually box, click on the Lower limit box and type in a new value 0 (zero); similarly, change the Upper value to 200. Then click on the **OK** button.
● Now see the effect.

Before moving on, look at the other line charts that are available. Two others are worth examination. Resize your chart area and move it to a blank area of your spreadsheet in preparation for the next section.

8.8 Scatter graphs or XY graphs

Such graphs are used to plot one variable against another in an attempt to see if there is any *correlation* or relationship between them. For example, in the line chart you have just produced, you plotted both number of claims and amount claimed against time. You could just as easily have plotted the number of claims against the amounts claimed to see if there is any relationship between these two variables. In this case, you will see that they tend to increase together.

Screen dump 8.11 shows such a graph that has been added to the sheet where the relationship can be seen. In such a case you simply plot one variable (X) against another variable (Y). Time does not matter in this case. In practice, such charts would be used with a much larger amount of data where the relationship might not be so obvious.

It can be seen that when the number of claims is high, so is the amount claimed, demonstrating a positive correlation. Another relationship could be the opposite, for example, if you were to plot rainfall against temperature, you might find that on days when rainfall is high, there is a tendency for temperatures to be lower. This is called negative correlation.

Where there is correlation between two variables, it is possible to use such relationships to predict events. For example, if there is correlation of a positive kind between temperature and rainfall, you could work out the likely average temperature given a certain amount of rainfall. Lotus 1-2-3 has an Advanced Maths utility that can assist here; a topic beyond the scope of a book of this nature.

- Highlight the range K7..L18.
- Draw a new chart area as you have done before.

You will see that Lotus makes an instant attempt to draw a chart for you and should have defaulted to a Line chart (this is dependent on the last chart type you created).

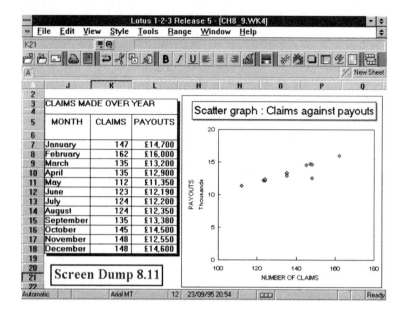

CLAIMS MADE OVER YEAR

MONTH	CLAIMS	PAYOUTS
January	147	£14,700
February	162	£16,000
March	135	£13,200
April	135	£12,900
May	112	£11,350
June	123	£12,190
July	124	£12,200
August	124	£12,350
September	135	£13,380
October	145	£14,500
November	148	£12,550
December	148	£14,600

Screen Dump 8.11

- Click on the Chart Type SmartIcon and click on XY.

Look back at **Screen dump 8.3** and on the basis of this give your chart appropriate titles and remove any legend boxes.

You will see a set of six possible charts of this kind. The one in **Screen dump 8.11** is the bottom right where the plotted points are not joined. This technically, is the right choice for a scatter chart.

- Click on the appropriate XY chart and look at your chart.

Resize and move the chart to an appropriate part of the spreadsheet.

Before moving on to the final section, try experimenting with this chart to see the effect that changing the data might have. In experimenting with the chart try the following:

- Create numbers in the table such that as the number of claims increase the amounts claimed decrease.
- Randomise the figures so that there is no apparent correlation between them.

8.9 Geographic maps

This facility is only available for Release 5 and later users. Lotus 1-2-3 has a facility whereby you can draw and label maps for areas of the world. Observe **Screen dump 8.12** to see what can be achieved with only a few commands.

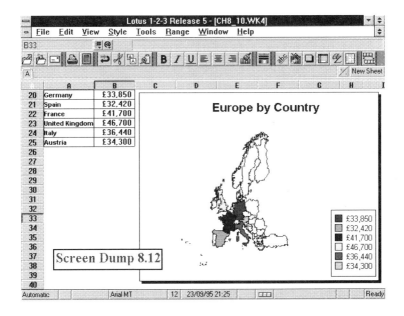

- To create such a map, go to a part of the spreadsheet that is blank or create a new spreadsheet.
- In the top left of your screen, type in a table of the six countries. Rather than enter United Kingdom in the fourth row, enter England. Type in the numbers in the second column.

The map that will be drawn will be taken from a database within the Lotus 1-2-3 program. Part of the program also has the ability of identifying which country names belong to which map; as will now be demonstrated.

- Highlight the whole table: the country names and numbers.
- Click on <u>T</u>ools, then <u>M</u>ap, then <u>N</u>ew map.

A Map Type dialogue box will now appear listing all the regions of the world for which Lotus 1-2-3 has a map.

- Select Europe by Country from the list that appears in the <u>S</u>elect a map box.

If you entered England as one of the countries, Lotus 1-2-3 will not recognise it as a country. It will, however, recognise United Kingdom. Another example could be if Holland was in your list; Lotus 1-2-3 would require Netherlands instead. If this is not acceptable to you, then you can have the country name you have entered swapped with the one that comes with Lotus 1-2-3.

- If the Region check dialogue box has appeared, then select the correct country from the Known map region box, then click on the **OK** button.
- A small icon appears of the world globe spinning. Position this on your spreadsheet, click your mouse button and position and size the map on your screen.

You should now have the desired effect. The map, with its legends, is a floating object in the same way as a chart. You can, if you wish, alter the features of the chart by clicking on <u>T</u>ools, then ma<u>p</u> and selecting a range of options from there.

——— 8.10 Chapter summary ———

This chapter has set out to cover many of the chart and map creation aspects of Lotus 1-2-3. It has not covered everything available and will leave you to investigate other aspects more fully.

In this chapter you have:

- determined an X and a Y axis.
- set up a simple bar chart.
- constructed a multiple bar chart.
- entered titles and legends on a chart.
- altered the perspective of a chart.
- constructed a stack bar chart.
- constructed pie charts.

- added annotated objects to a chart.
- constructed lines charts with single and multiple variables.
- constructed three-dimensional charts.
- altered the scaling of an axis.
- constructed scatter diagrams.
- created a labelled map.

9

THREE-DIMENSIONAL SPREADSHEETS

───── 9.1 Aims of this chapter ─────

This chapter will introduce you to the idea of working with multiple spreadsheets. Lotus 1-2-3 refers to the concept as 3-D, or three-dimensional.

The principle is that a spreadsheet has columns and rows and so is two-dimensional. A third dimension is added when you have a stack of sheets one on top of another. Lotus 1-2-3 will allow you to have 256 such sheets, although filling all these up will be restricted by the amount of memory available. The idea works rather like a book, in that a single page of the book reads across and down, while a whole series of sheets make up a book.

With respect to the spreadsheet, each layer will be called a sheet and the whole collection of these sheets will be called the spreadsheet.

In earlier chapters you have come across the idea of having more than one spreadsheet open at any one time. You can cascade the display of spreadsheets to create a layered effect similar to what you will see in this chapter. The difference, however, is that each sheet in a multi-layered spreadsheet is permanently connected and they will all load when the spreadsheet is open. It will also be considerably easier to link formulae in one sheet with data stored on another.

— 9.2 Looking at multiple sheets —

Begin with a blank sheet displayed on your screen.

● Click on <u>V</u>iew from the pull-down menu, then click on <u>S</u>plit and from the resulting dialogue box, set the <u>P</u>erspective mode on.

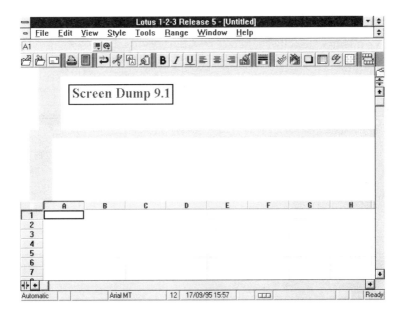

Screen Dump 9.1

At this stage you will see three sheets on your screen similar to those shown in **Screen dump 9.1**. The sheet in front is labelled Sheet 'A' and is the only active sheet in the spreadsheet. This chapter will require you to work with four sheets to show you how Lotus 1-2-3 works in this three-dimensional environment.

● Click on <u>E</u>dit from the pull-down menu, then Insert option and, in the dialogue box, click on <u>S</u>heet.
● Now click on <u>A</u>fter (to indicate that you want the sheets to appear after A. Namely B, C and D), and set <u>Q</u>uantity to 3.
● When done, click on **OK**.

Screen dump 9.2 shows B, C, D displayed at the same time. As you will observe, they are all labelled with row numbers and column letters. The perspective view of the spreadsheet will show exactly three sheets at a time; Sheet A has not been lost.

Although you have selected four sheets you will see later in this chapter that you can always add or delete sheets to and from these and place them or delete them before, after and between other sheets, rather like adding or removing pages in a loose-leaf book.

The highlighted cell should now be A1 of sheet B. The cell indicator in the control panel refers to this cell as B:A1. As a useful tip, think of cell A:A1 as being directly in front and cell C:A1 as directly behind.

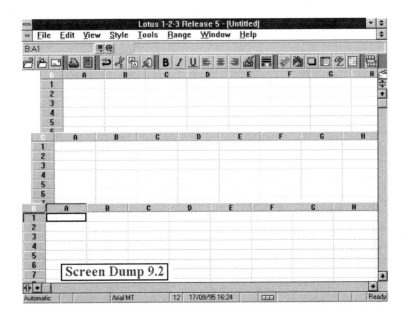

Screen Dump 9.2

- Press down **Ctrl** and press **Page Up** to move to sheet C.
- Now hold down the **Ctrl** key and press the **Page Down** key to move back to sheet B, then to sheet A. (You will observe that sheet D no longer appears on your screen.)

Within each sheet the right, left, up and down arrow keys are used to navigate within a sheet. Experiment further with moving between sheets and within sheets until you are familiar with the idea.

You should now see what is meant by the concept of a three-dimensional spreadsheet. We now have columns with letter headings A, B, C, D...., rows with numbers 1, 2, 3, 4, 5... and layers of sheets A:, B:, C:, D: ... The next stage is to see what can be done with this extra dimension.

—— 9.3 Setting up the first sheet ——

This example will begin by setting up sheet A with a Sales Analysis table for Europa Components to different countries in the month of October. When building up any single sheet, working with the perspective mode on will prove awkward because you can only view six lines in a sheet, so you will need to clear this when making up a sheet.

- Using the **Ctrl** and **Page Down** keys make sure that the current working sheet is within Sheet A:.
- Now click on <u>V</u>iew, then Clear <u>S</u>plit.

On the screen you will see a set of worksheet tabs A, B, C and D just above the spreadsheet area. You can use these to skip between sheets by clicking the relevant sheet.

Although you will only see one sheet in the conventional way, you need to bear in mind that the other sheets (B, C and D) are still resident. It is rather like having a book open at a particular page and only being able to see that page in spite of the others still being there.

- Type in the labels:

label	cell
'EUROPA COMPONENTS'	A1
'Sales Analysis by Country'	A3
'OCTOBER'	C3
'Country'	A5
'Sales'	B5
'Value'	B6
'Percentage'	C5

- Widen columns, where necessary. And make the title and labels more prominent.
- Type in the 9 countries in the range of cells A8 to16 as they appear in **Screen dump 9.3**.

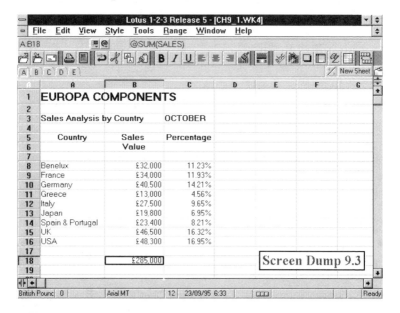

Screen Dump 9.3

- Highlight column B, click on your left mouse button while the pointer is on the range, and use the Number Format option to set the figures to Currency.
- Type in a set of sales values in the range B8..B16 as shown in **Screen dump 9.3**.
- Highlight the range of sales values in B8 to B16 and, click on Range, then Name the range as SALES.
- Now click on cell B18 and type in the function @SUM(SALES).
- The formula in cell C8 is +B8/B$18. Type this in and note how the row location of 18 in the formula has been fixed as absolute. This will permit copying.
- Now format this cell to percent and to 2 decimal places.
- Ensuring the cell pointer is at cell C8, click on the Copy SmartIcon to place the formula in the Clipboard.
- Now highlight the range of cells C9 to C16 and click on the Paste SmartIcon to paste the formula into each of the cells in the range.

- Observe **Screen dump 9.3** to make sure that you have a similar set up.

—— 9.4 Copying between sheets ——

Your next objective will be to copy the entire contents of Sheet A on to Sheet B. The principle is no different from copying from a range of cells to another in the same sheet.

- Highlight all the cells in the range A1 to C18 and, click on the Copy SmartIcon to place a copy of the details into the Clipboard.
- Click on the View, then Split and set the Perspective mode back on.
- Now click on cell A1 of Sheet B.

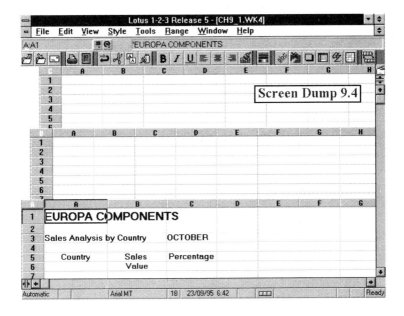

Screen dump 9.4 shows the effect where the cursor is positioned in sheet B and you are ready to copy the contents of sheet A into this.

You can also jump to Sheet B by pressing the function key **F5** and entering the cell location B:A1.

Ensure the cursor is in A1 in sheet B and click on the Paste SmartIcon.

The end result of this was to copy from A:A1..C8 to B:A1. You now have an identical copy of the sheets in both parts of the spreadsheet. However, you will have a problem in that the two sheets have different column widths and the data will not fit into the cells correctly in Sheet B. You will now have to set the *Group mode* on.

- Click on <u>S</u>tyle, then click on <u>W</u>orksheet Defaults. In the dialogue box is a box headed Other. Make sure the <u>G</u>roup mode box has an X.

- Click on **OK** and you will see that this solves the problem immediately.

9.5 Entering three-dimensional formulae

- Make sure you are in sheet B and remove the perspective, by clicking on <u>V</u>iew, then Clear <u>S</u>plit.

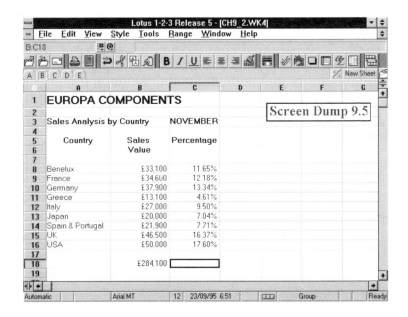

- Examine **Screen dump 9.5** and make the necessary alterations to the label in C3 by altering the month to NOVEMBER and then type in new sales values in the range B8 to B16.

You will now type into Sheet B a formula that works out the difference between sales in the current month of November and those of the previous month of October, in other words the differences of the values in the two cells of B6.

- First, alter the column width of column D. (Because the Group mode is set enabled, it will automatically set the column widths of all sheets.)
- Type in the new column heading of sales change so that 'Sales change' appears in D5 and 'on Month' appears in D6. Also centre and embolden this new heading.

Now you are ready to use a formula that links with the other sheet.

- In cell D8 type in the formula +B8-A:B8.

Cell B8 contains the monthly sales for Benelux in the current sheet for November. Cell A:B8 is in sheet A, as its prefix implies, and contains the Benelux sales for October. The formula calculates the difference in sales between the two months. A negative figure implies a fall in sales between the two months; a positive one showing an increase.

Now you will need to do the same for the remaining countries. Because the relative position of the remaining countries all remain the same, you will be able to copy and paste the formula already entered to the remaining countries.

- Click on cell D8, click on the Copy SmartIcon.
- Highlight cells D9 to D16 and, click on the Paste SmartIcon.
- Now type in the totalling function in cell D18: @SUM(D8..D16).
- Set the range of numbers D8 to D18 to currency and to zero decimal places.

Examine **Screen dump 9.6** to see Sheet B as something with a more interesting appearance.

- Develop the Style of Sheet B as though it was the only sheet in use. (Do not be too concerned at getting an exact likeness.)
- Click on the worksheet tabs to move between sheets.

Observe how the style settings have been created in all sheets.

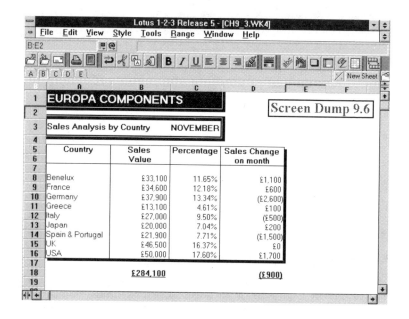

9.6 Building up a history

The next stage is to copy the contents of Sheet B to Sheet C to give sales for December.

- Highlight the entire range (cells A1 to D18) of sheet B, then click on the Copy SmartIcon.
- Click on the Sheet C tab and then click on A1 in sheet C.
- Click on the Paste SmartIcon.

Screen dump 9.7 shows the likely result with the Styles all done for you as well.

Screen Dump 9.7

EUROPA COMPONENTS

Sales Analysis by Country   NOVEMBER

Country	Sales Value	Percentage	Sales Change on month
Benelux	£33,100	11.65%	£0
France	£34,600	12.18%	£0
Germany	£37,900	13.34%	£0
Greece	£13,100	4.61%	£0
Italy	£27,000	9.50%	£0
Japan	£20,000	7.04%	£0
Spain & Portugal	£21,900	7.71%	£0
UK	£46,500	16.37%	£0
USA	£50,000	17.60%	£0
	£284,100		**£0**

You will notice that the 'Sales change on month' columns shows all zeros. This is exactly to be expected because monthly figures in both Sheet B and Sheet C are at present the same. This confirms that the formulae have been copied successfully as well as the numbers and labels.

- Make sure you are working in Sheet C.
- Alter the label in C3 to DECEMBER.
- Using the data shown in **Screen dump 9.8**, type in a new set of monthly sales figures for the countries and observe what happens to the figures in the column 'Sales Change on month' as you work through it.

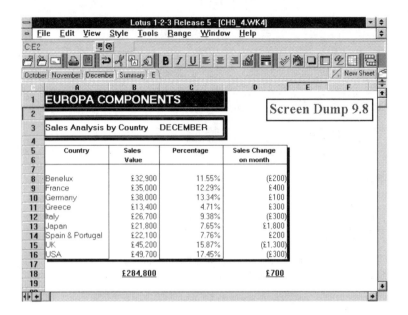

The percentage figures will also change as the new sales values are typed in. However, these are based on two-dimensional formulae.

You will notice that the tabs have been labelled. To achieve this:

● double click on the tab you want to label, then type in the new label. (The summary tab can be added after the next section.)

You should now be able to appreciate that the task becomes easier as you work through the months. You may, for example, want to go on with this for many more months. With a maximum of 256 sheets in a spreadsheet, this allows for over 21 years of data!

—— 9.7 Summarising the sheets ——

The next task is to produce a summary sheet that adds all the monthly sales figures together. You could enter this, for example, as Sheet Z, giving yourself room for many more months after December. However, this is unnecessary as you will always have the opportunity to insert sheets between existing ones in the same way as you would insert a new column or row within a single sheet.

Screen dump 9.9 shows the desired effect where the Sales Value figures are the totals for each of the three months you have already entered on Sheets A, B and C.

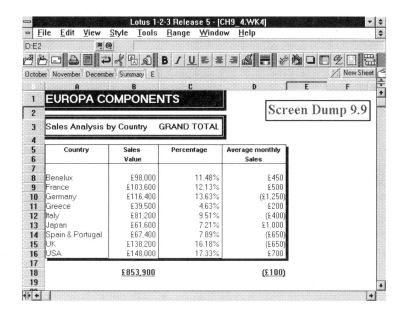

The figures in column B will sum up all monthly sales from October to December, and Column D will calculate the average sales for each country over the three months. In both cases, the formulae will be calculated on figures across more than one sheet.

- Copy the entire contents of sheet C to sheet D without using the perspective screen set-up.
- In Sheet D, alter the label in C3 to: GRAND TOTAL.
- Alter the label in D5 to: Average monthly and D6 to: Sales.

- Highlight cells B8 to B16 and press the **Delete** key.
- Highlight cells D8 to D16 and press the **Delete** key.
- Click on cell B8 and type in the formula @SUM(A:B8..C:B8).

- Copy the function in B8 to range B9 to B16.
- Label the sheet D tab as Summary.

The function in cell B8 has added together the contents of the three values in B8 for Sheets A (October), B (November) and C (December), in a three-dimensional sense. It would now be easy to add another sheet for another month between the sheets for December and Summary and then include this extra month in the formula. Simply staying in the Summary sheet and inserting a new sheet would have the desired effect.

As a further demonstration of how the three-dimensional effect works, you will calculate a formula that works out the average monthly sales value of the three months' sales value figures.

- Click on cell D8 and type in the function @AVG(A:B8..C:B8).
- Now copy this formula from cell D8 to cells D9 to D16.

You now have two sets of formulae that make use of the three-dimensional effect. If you are unsure as to what has happened, then browse through the range of cells where the formulae have been set to see how it has worked.

In order to gain a better appreciation of this, insert a sheet for the month of January.

- Click on <u>E</u>dit, then <u>I</u>nsert, then <u>S</u>heet, then <u>B</u>efore, then click on the **OK** button.
- Label the new tab as January.
- Now copy the contents of December to January and make amendments to the text in C3 and the Sales Values.

Make the necessary alterations to the formulae in the Summary sheet which should, after the insertion, be Sheet E.

—— **9.8 Adding a fourth dimension** ——

This chapter has covered the idea of multiple sheets for the 12 different months. After one year has lapsed, the whole process really ought to start again. In this instance you would create another sheet on the lines of what has already been achieved. To do this easily, you could create a new spreadsheet and copy the previous year's sheets into it.

The rest of this chapter now assumes that you have added a new month of January. This is now Sheet D while the summary sheet is in Sheet E.

- Click on File, then Save As, and save the sheet as YEAR1.
- Repeat this but save the spreadsheet as YEAR2.
- Now open the YEAR1 sheet by clicking File and then on 1 YEAR1 in the list of files at the bottom of the file menu.
- Click on Window, then Cascade, so that you are able to see your two spreadsheets; one on top of the other.

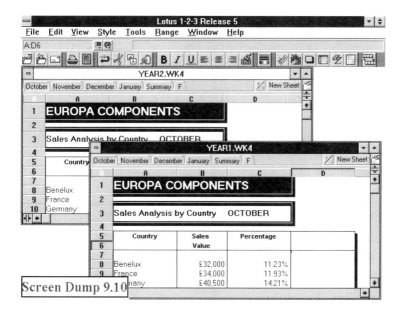

Screen Dump 9.10

Screen dump 9.10 shows the cascade effect. The sheet can be moved around the working area in the same way as an object on a sheet. You can hop between spreadsheets by clicking on either of them.

- Click on YEAR2 and then click on the maximise button so that YEAR 1 is hidden from view.
- Go through each of the sheets October to January altering the sales figures to anything you wish.

● In the October sheet, type the label 'Sales Change' in cell E5 and 'on year' in cell E6.

Screen dump 9.11 shows the result you will be aiming for where each month's figures are compared with the same month in the previous year.

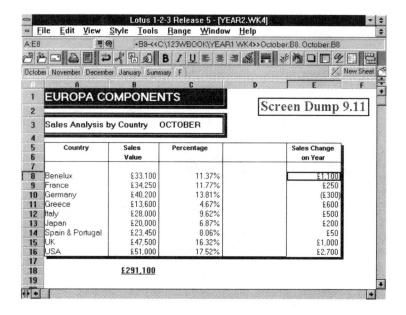

The identification of another spreadsheet in a formula is done by placing the complete file name between << and >> (In other words, two 'less than' symbols and two 'greater than' symbols).

The formula in cell E8 needs to be subtracted from A:B8 the value in the YEAR1 sheet. Knowing that the sheet where the number is stored is YEAR1.WK4, the formula needs to be prefixed with this name. That is: <<YEAR1.WK4>>. However, an easier way would be to make better use of your mouse and the window facility available.

● Click on Window, then Tile.
● Make sure that both spreadsheets are in October *and* cells E8 are both visible.

- Click on cell E8 in the YEAR2 spreadsheet.
- Press the + (plus) key; do not press **Enter** yet.
- Now click on cell B8 from the same sheet and then press the – (minus) key; again, do not press **Enter** yet.
- Now click on cell B8 in the YEAR1 spreadsheet.
- Press the **Enter** key and you will have the desired result.
- Close the YEAR1 spreadsheet and maximise YEAR2.
- Copy cell B8 to the range B9 to B16.

The power of this should now be clear to see, where you can even copy the formula.

- Highlight cells E8 to E16, then click on the Copy SmartIcon.
- Move to cell E8 in the November Sheet and click on the Paste SmartIcon.
- Now repeat this for the other sheets.
- Now save the current sheet as YEAR2.

9.9 Chapter summary

In this chapter you have concentrated on creating and manipulating a three-dimensional spreadsheet. However, this has the advantage of leaving you with only one spreadsheet to concern yourself with in terms of file handling and presents you with easier formulae when working in three dimensions.

In this chapter you have:

- created extra sheets in a spreadsheet to create a three-dimensional effect.
- viewed and moved between multiple sheets.
- set up the Group mode and performed Style set ups for all sheets.
- typed data into one sheet and copied it to another.
- typed formulae and functions into a sheet that are derived from data in other sheets.
- opened another spreadsheet and worked with two multiple sheet spreadsheets.
- linked spreadsheets with the <<FILENAME>> facility.

10

SAMPLE EXERCISES

10.1 Aims of this chapter

This book has introduced you to a large variety of the possible applications of spreadsheets. This chapter offers further ideas for spreadsheet use.

In addition, some exercises will help develop your skills further with Lotus 1-2-3 for Windows. If you work through the exercises in sequence, you will find that they become gradually more demanding.

10.2 Selling soft toys

1 Load your spreadsheet and type in the title 'EXPENSE DETAILS FOR HARRY'S SOFT TOYS' in the first row. On the third row type in the author's name (yours) along with the date the spreadsheet is generated.

2 Generating today's date requires the @TODAY function followed by formatting the cell. Formatting the date is available in the Style pull down menu as Number Format.

3 Type in rows 6 to 11, as shown in **Screen dump 10.1**.

4 In cell A13 type in the label TOTAL (right justify this by typing "TOTAL).

5 Now type in a formula in cell B13 that calculates the sum of values in the range B7 to B11.

6 Copy the formula from cell B13 to cells C13 to E13.

7 In columns F and G type in data for MAY and JUNE.

	MAY	JUNE
WAGES	455	495
RENT	80	80
RATES	190	190
HEATING	15	18
SUNDRIES	26	33

8 In column H type in the heading TOTAL.

9 In cell H7 type in a formula that totals the expenses for each category. Copy this formula from H7 to cells H8 to H11.

10 Copy the formula in cell E13 to cells F13 to H13.

11 Incorrect information has been collected on the costs of sundries, which should be 20 in February and 25 in April. Adjust the amounts accordingly to recalculate the total costs.

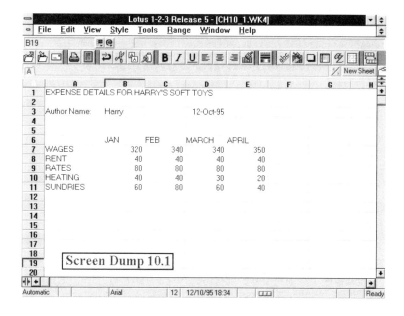

Screen Dump 10.1

12 Format all numeric cells so that they are displayed in currency format to zero decimal places.

13 Add a new row at row 15. In cell A15 give it the title INCOME followed by the following sales income values for each month:

	Jan	Feb	Mar	Apr	May	Jun
Sales Income	2,000	3,000	3,000	4,000	5,000	5,000

14 Now add a final row called SURPLUS and under the JAN column type in a formula that shows the surplus value as being: (Sales Income) minus (Total Cost). Copy this formula across the spreadsheet.

15 Check that all numeric formats are in currency and make any adjustments you feel necessary to tidy up the presentation of your spreadsheet.

16 Experiment with some of the Lotus fonts to improve the style of your spreadsheet.

17 Print the entire spreadsheet, remembering to define the range you want printed first.

18 Save your work with the file name HARRY.

——— 10.3 Arnold's fish bar ———

1 Load up your spreadsheet package and type in your name and today's date at the top of the spreadsheet. Remember, the @TODAY function can be used for this as described in Chapter 6.

2 Type in a title on row 3: ARNOLD'S FISH BAR SALES.

3 Widen column A.

4 Set up the spreadsheet with the labels shown in **Screen dump 10.2a** with the column headings starting on row 5 and the row headings in column A.

5 The numbers that appear in the spreadsheet should also be typed in. Make sure that your text is left justified and numbers right justified.

6 Generate the INCOME obtained from COD by multiplying the PRICE by the number SOLD and putting the answer in the INCOME column.

7 On row 14 use a formula to calculate the total items MADE, the total dishes SOLD and the total INCOME.

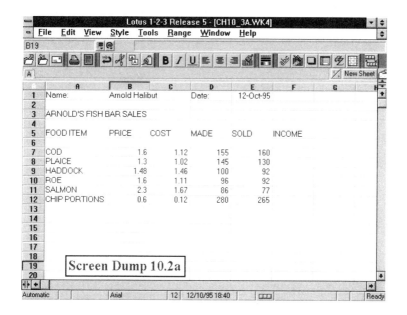

Screen Dump 10.2a

8 Add an extra column to the spreadsheet to show the profit made on each dish. Under the heading PROFIT generate the data for each dish using the formula:

$$PROFIT = INCOME - (COST * MADE)$$

9 Format all money values to currency.

10 Now change the numeric data to the ones shown in **Screen dump 10.2b** to check that your spreadsheet still calculates the INCOME, PROFIT and TOTALS correctly with the new figures.

11 Produce two more columns with the column headings UNSOLD to hold the column of stock for each item that was left unsold (MADE-SOLD), and a column headed WASTE to hold the cost to the fish bar of this unsold stock (UNSOLD * COST).

12 Zoom out so that all data is in view on your screen and then compare the outcome with that shown in Screen dump 10.2b.

13 Make any alterations to the presentation required and save your spreadsheet.

14 Print out this spreadsheet.

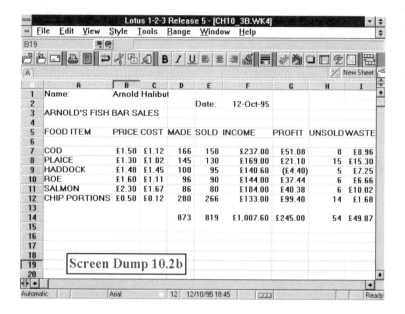

	A	B	C	D	E	F	G	H	I
1	Name:	Arnold Halibut							
2				Date:	12-Oct-95				
3	ARNOLD'S FISH BAR SALES								
4									
5	FOOD ITEM	PRICE	COST	MADE	SOLD	INCOME	PROFIT	UNSOLD	WASTE
6									
7	COD	£1.50	£1.12	166	158	£237.00	£51.08	8	£8.96
8	PLAICE	£1.30	£1.02	145	130	£169.00	£21.10	15	£15.30
9	HADDOCK	£1.48	£1.45	100	95	£140.60	(£4.40)	5	£7.25
10	ROE	£1.60	£1.11	96	90	£144.00	£37.44	6	£6.66
11	SALMON	£2.30	£1.67	86	80	£184.00	£40.38	6	£10.02
12	CHIP PORTIONS	£0.50	£0.12	280	266	£133.00	£99.40	14	£1.68
13									
14				873	819	£1,007.60	£245.00	54	£49.87
15									
16									
17									
18									
19	**Screen Dump 10.2b**								
20									

10.4 An electricity bill

This exercise requires you to set up a model electricity bill similar to that shown in **Screen dump 10.3**. If you have an electricity bill of your own to use, then model it around this instead.

When you set out this spreadsheet, bear in mind the following formulae:

- No. of units = (Current meter reading) - (Last meter reading)
- Total Cost for units in £ = (No.of Units) * (Cost per Unit in pence) / 100
- VAT = (VAT Rate) * (Total Cost for Units + Standing Charge)
- TOTAL NOW DUE = (Total Cost for Units) + (Standing Charge) + VAT

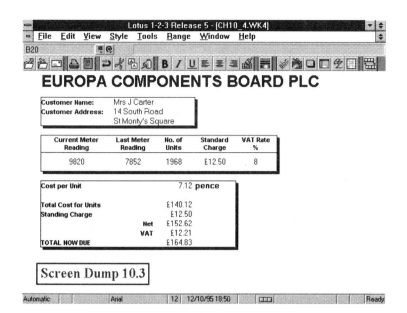

When you complete the exercise, experiment with a few bills with different meter readings to convince yourself that the spreadsheet works correctly.

10.5 Calorie control

The following exercise is an example of how a spreadsheet can be used to give instant and accurate measures of the number of calories contained within a specific diet. When working through it, you ought to consider how it can be extended to include other variables such as certain vitamins.

The spreadsheet is split into two parts: one contains the ACTUAL DIET of a given patient, while the other contains the CALORIE CONTROL CHART. Basically, the spreadsheet will collect the details of the patient from a user and then calculate the calories consumed in the diet by reading these details from the Calorie Control Chart.

Calorie control chart

The chart will need to go somewhere on the spreadsheet where it is out of the way, as this data will be standard and does not need to be changed too often. The ideal place would be to create a second Sheet as B.

1 Insert one sheet after the current one.
2 Turn the Group mode off because you will not want formats and column widths to be the same throughout.
3 Start at position B:A1 and type the details as shown in **Screen dump 10.4a** which will hold the calorie content per 100 grams of a range of food and drink.

When generating this table, you will need to adjust the column widths to fit the data.

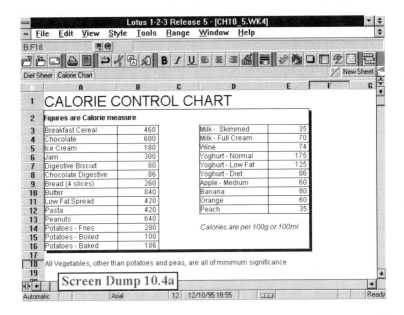

4 Change the look of the sheet. (Remove grid lines, add a border, colour, etc.)
5 Print out the chart. (You will need to specify the range you want printed prior to its actual printing.)

Patient diet sheet

6 Return to Sheet A.

7 Type in a patient diet sheet for a given day, starting at position A1, to look something like that set out in **Screen dumps 10.4b and 10.4c.** You will observe that the spreadsheet exceeds the number of lines that can fit on to one screen. You can, of course, Zoom Out to fit it all on to one screen, but it will be hard to read.

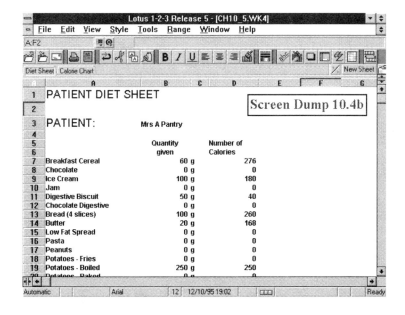

Column C has been used to indicate the unit of measure. It is important that you do not put this in Column B, as it would make the values non-numeric. The effect is, therefore, to allow you to use the quantities to perform some calculations with.

8 Be careful to create a column C for the unit of measure (g or ml) and narrow the column. Column B will be used to store the numbers.

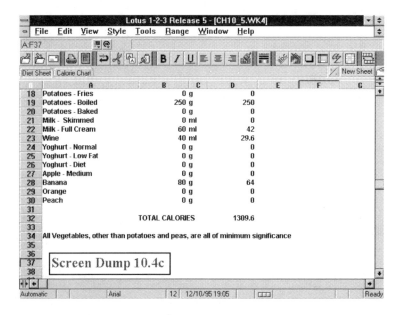

	A	B	C	D	E	F	G
18	Potatoes - Fries		0 g	0			
19	Potatoes - Boiled		250 g	250			
20	Potatoes - Baked		0 g	0			
21	Milk - Skimmed		0 ml	0			
22	Milk - Full Cream		60 ml	42			
23	Wine		40 ml	29.6			
24	Yoghurt - Normal		0 g	0			
25	Yoghurt - Low Fat		0 g	0			
26	Yoghurt - Diet		0 g	0			
27	Apple - Medium		0 g	0			
28	Banana		80 g	64			
29	Orange		0 g	0			
30	Peach		0 g	0			
31							
32		TOTAL CALORIES		1309.6			
33							
34	All Vegetables, other than potatoes and peas, are all of minimum significance						
35							
36							
37	**Screen Dump 10.4c**						
38							

9 Make sure that the entries of the NUMBER OF CALORIES are found and calculated by the computer. For example, the number for Full Cream Milk in cell location D22 is calculated as follows: Grams given, to be found in cell B22, divided by 100 and then multiplied by the number of calories per 100 millilitres which was placed into cell E4 of Sheet B. Consequently, for cell D22 the formula will need to read : +B22/100*B:E4.

10 Perform some of the finishing touches to improve the presentation of your work.

11 Finally, use the @SUM function to find the totals for this patient and then print the details of the patient's diet.

─── 10.6 Employee sickness ───

This exercise requires you to perform the following tasks:

1 Ensure you have started with a blank spreadsheet.

2 Enter text on to your spreadsheet to show a heading and a list of employee names as shown in **Screen dump 10.5**.

3 Type in, for each employee: number of days' sickness and the number of possible days they could have worked.
4 Type in dates From and To using the Lotus @DATE function.
5 Calculate the number of days between the two dates.

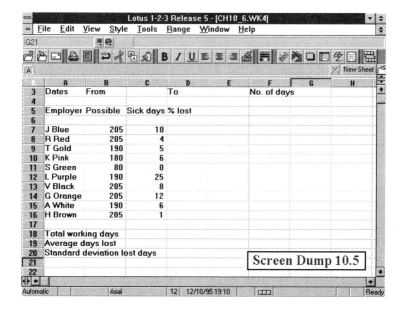

	A	B	C	D	E	F	G	H
3	Dates	From		To		No. of days		
4								
5	Employer	Possible	Sick days	% lost				
6								
7	J Blue	205	10					
8	R Red	205	4					
9	T Gold	190	5					
10	K Pink	180	6					
11	S Green	80	0					
12	L Purple	190	25					
13	V Black	205	8					
14	G Orange	205	12					
15	A White	190	6					
16	H Brown	205	1					
17								
18	Total working days							
19	Average days lost							
20	Standard deviation lost days							

Screen Dump 10.5

6 Calculate the percentage of days lost through sickness for each employee.
7 Now create NAMED ranges: possible days lost and percentage for columns B, C and D respectively. Paste a table of the named ranges similar to that shown in **Screen dump 10.5**.
8 Calculate total working days, total lost days, an average percentage of days' sickness and a standard deviation for sickness days.

Note: In order to tackle this Lotus 1-2-3 has an in-built function for the standard deviation: @STD(Percentage).

9 Smarten up the presentation.
10 Get a printout of the table you have generated.
11 Alter some of the sick days' figures and possible work days to make sure that the calculations work. Print out a second spreadsheet.

10.7 Price lists for a transport company

Examine **Screen dump 10.6**, showing a transport company's price list before starting this exercise.

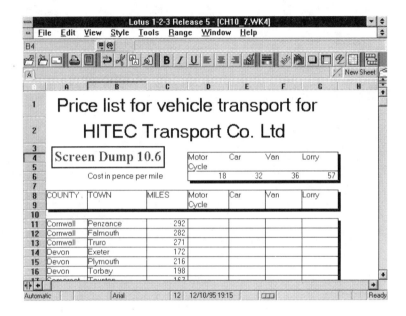

You will see that there is a heading for a county and for a town or city within that county. The mileage indicates the number of miles from the town to a fictitious London office.

The costs indicate the cost per mile for running each vehicle type. For each town, therefore, the cost of running a vehicle from London to the stated town is calculated. The use of such a spreadsheet allows a new price list to be easily and quickly constructed each time the prices per mile change.

1 Construct such a list for England, Scotland, Wales or any other country by having every county (or province or state) represented by between two and four principal towns or cities. You will need a map of the country with the mileage between the town or city and your chosen central location.

2 For each country, produce two lists with the following costs:

	first list	second list
Motor Cycle:	£0.18	£0.21
Car:	£0.32	£0.34
Van:	£0.36	£0.33
Truck:	£0.57	£0.55

The monetary values should be in currency format.

3 Rearrange your list using the Database Sort facilities into County (or Province or State) order and, within each county, organised in town or city order.

4 Save what you created in task 3 and produce the list in town order.

5 Repeat task 4 but rearrange the list into order of distance, with the farthest distance at the top of the list.

(The whole spreadsheet can be made visible on the screen by adjusting the column widths.)

——— 10.8 World weather chart ———

This spreadsheet sets out a world weather chart to show the temperature in different locations throughout the world. See **Screen dump 10.7**.

1 Design a spreadsheet to display this information. Include data taken from newspapers. The temperature in Fahrenheit should be calculated from the temperature in Centigrade by using the formula:

Fahrenheit = Centigrade *1.8 + 32.

2 At the foot of your table, show:

The average temperature
The number of locations

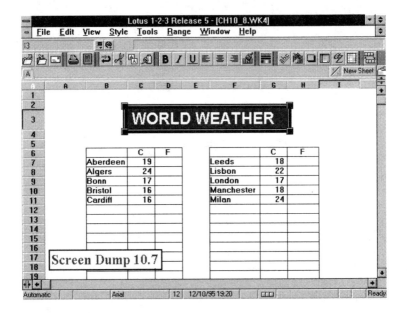

The name of the hottest place
The name of the coldest place

These figures should be determined using the Lotus 1-2-3 functions and not simply entered.

3 Print the table.
4 Alter the temperatures.

— 10.9 Car Burglar alarm explosion —

This spreadsheet requires you to set out the components of a car burglar alarm system that is to be produced by a small engineering company. The final product will be in black box form, ready to install in a car. The objective of this exercise is to calculate, at component level, the cost of materials and production of the alarm in order to derive a profitable selling price.

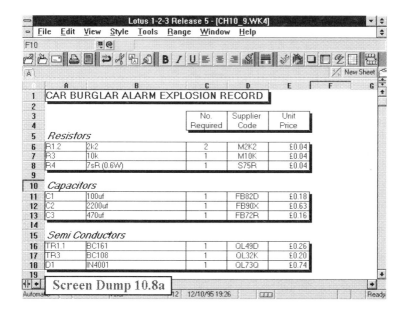

Screen Dump 10.8a

From the list shown in **Screen dumps 10.8a and 10.8b**, you should be able to enter the number of alarm systems you wish to make. The spreadsheet will then produce a 'shopping list', giving a list of the components needed and their costs, along with a total cost. It is suggested, therefore, that your spreadsheet has the following sections:

● A component breakdown as shown in **Screen dump 10.8a**.

Then add to the spreadsheet the following details:

● A column to hold costs of multiple components; e.g. 10 x R1.2 resistors 2K2.

● An entry for the desired number of 'final product' car alarm(s).

● A list of total components needed, with unit costs, in alphabetical order.

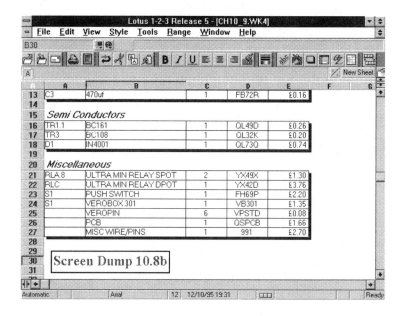

	A	B	C	D	E	F	G
13	C3	470uf	1	FB72R	£0.16		
14							
15	*Semi Conductors*						
16	TR1.1	BC161	1	QL49D	£0.26		
17	TR3	BC108	1	QL32K	£0.20		
18	D1	IN4001	1	QL73Q	£0.74		
19							
20	*Miscellaneous*						
21	RLA.8	ULTRA MIN RELAY SPOT	2	YX49X	£1.30		
22	RLC	ULTRA MIN RELAY DPOT	1	YX42D	£3.76		
23	S1	PUSH SWITCH	1	FH69P	£2.20		
24	S1	VEROBOX 301	1	VB301	£1.35		
25		VEROPIN	6	VPSTD	£0.08		
26		PCB	1	QSPCB	£1.66		
27		MISC WIRE/PINS	1	991	£2.70		
28							
29							
30	**Screen Dump 10.8b**						
31							

Try taking advantage of macros in order to sort the list by costs as well as in component order. Also, use a macro to simplify the printing of each section.

You will find the use of a horizontal window valuable because the spreadsheet has more rows of information than can be seen on the screen at any one time.

10.10 League tables

This spreadsheet is designed to show a football league championship table, and can easily be adapted to suit any league-based sport. The table has been sorted so that the club with the highest number of points appears at the top. When two clubs have the same number of points, the order is by goal difference.

Part of the table takes the form of the one shown in **Screen dump 10.9**.

The point system assumed is:

Win = 3 points
Draw = 1 point

Games Played = Won + Lost + Drawn
Goal Difference = (goals for) - (goals against)

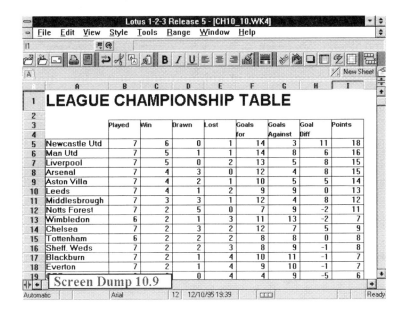

		Lotus 1-2-3 Release 5 - [CH10_10.WK4]						

File Edit View Style Tools Range Window Help

LEAGUE CHAMPIONSHIP TABLE

	A	B	C	D	E	F	G	H	I
3		Played	Win	Drawn	Lost	Goals for	Goals Against	Goal Diff	Points
5	Newcastle Utd	7	6	0	1	14	3	11	18
6	Man Utd	7	5	1	1	14	8	6	16
7	Liverpool	7	5	0	2	13	5	8	15
8	Arsenal	7	4	3	0	12	4	8	15
9	Aston Villa	7	4	2	1	10	5	5	14
10	Leeds	7	4	1	2	9	9	0	13
11	Middlesbrough	7	3	3	1	12	4	8	12
12	Notts Forest	7	2	5	0	7	9	-2	11
13	Wimbledon	6	2	1	3	11	13	-2	7
14	Chelsea	7	2	3	2	12	7	5	9
15	Tottenham	6	2	2	2	8	8	0	8
16	Sheff. Weds	7	2	2	3	8	9	-1	8
17	Blackburn	7	2	1	4	10	11	-1	7
18	Everton	7	2	1	4	9	10	-1	7
19				0	4	4	9	-5	6

Screen Dump 10.9

Automatic | Arial | 12 | 12/10/95 19:39 | | Ready

1 Produce a spreadsheet for this table. You could take details from a league table listed in the sports section of a newspaper.
2 At the foot of the table show the following:

Number of clubs
Highest number of wins
Highest number of defeats
Average number of goals for
Average number of goals against
The average goal difference

All these figures should be shown to the nearest whole figure.

— 10.11 Hayley Computer Services —

This problem involves the setting up of a simple cash budget depicting a cash flow for a company. The pro-forma set out in **Screen dump 10.10** is designed to help you get started with the problem.

Hayley Computer Services Ltd is a small company offering computer consultancy and professional training to small businesses. The company has been trading for two years, the only staff being Mr James and his wife. Mr James is now worried that the £5,000 overdraft facility granted by his bank will be insufficient to finance his company's modest expansion. To assist in his investigation of several possible plans, he has decided to set up a cash flow model covering the next 12 months.

Mrs James has made the following estimates for the year ending December 31:

- Fees received by the company in January will be £2,900 and these will rise steadily by 5% per month.

Expenses of the company are expected to be:

- Rent for premises is £400 per month, fixed at this amount for the year.
- General expenses of £500 in January, rising steadily by 3% a month.
- Fixed motor vehicle expenses of £120 per month.
- Wages and tax of £1,800 a month, fixed for 6 months but increased from July onwards by 25%.

In March Mr James intends changing his company car. He believes that he will be able to sell his present car for £5,600 and that the replacement will cost £7,900.

In September he expects to pay tax of £5,920 on the company's previous year's profits.

On 1 January the company's bank account is expected to be £3,100 overdrawn.

1 Set up the model of the company's cash flow for the 12 months to December. You have the pro-forma set out in **Screen dump 10.10**

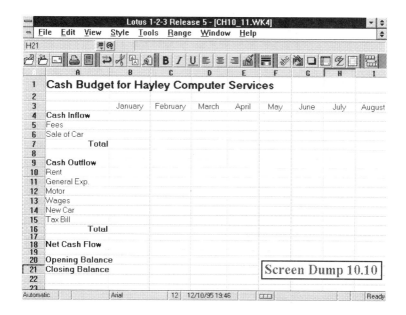

Screen Dump 10.10

to help you get started. All figures should be displayed to the nearest whole figure.

2 By modifying the basic model, ascertain the effect of each of the following proposals in turn on the company's overdraft position, so that Mr James can decide which option most favours his bank balance:

(a) A new issue of shares to Mr James' uncle, giving a cash inflow of £4,500 in February.

b) Taking out a loan of £4,000 in January to be repaid in December plus interest of £450;

c) Deferring the purchase of the new car for 12 months but facing extra running expenses of £40 a month after March.

d) Paying £1,000 for advertising in January with an increase in sales of £250 a month (over and above the 5% growth) beginning in February. Also vacating his rented premises and working at home from January.

10.12 The Rapid Cook Microwave Company

This problem requires you to design a Cash Budget similar to that of Exercise 10.11. However, the problems are more demanding and you are given less help with the initial layout.

A group of partners are to set up a limited company for the purpose of manufacturing and selling microwave ovens, with a start-up Share Capital of £60,000 in the bank on 1 June and an anticipated injection of further Share Capital from new shareholders once the business is underway.

The plans for the company are as follows:

● It will produce 120 ovens a month starting in June, but expects sales to start from 60 in July, increasing in steps of 20 each month until they reach 140 per month.

● The ovens will sell for £320 each with customer accounts being settled in the second month after the month of purchase.

● The overheads will be fixed at £5,000 per month, paid one month in arrears.

● In September the business will pay £150,000 for machinery and computers needed to start up the business.

● In November the extra injection of capital is expected. This amount should be £75,000.

● The unit (variable) production costs, which are not expected to rise in the period under review, will be as follows:

Materials	£90
Labour	£80
Variable Overheads	£40

Materials will be bought as needed with payments one month later. Labour will have to be paid in the month in which the expense is incurred, as will variable overheads.

● Interest on the previous month's overdraft is to be charged at 1.5% plus a £10 standing charge by the bank.

In order to satisfy the bank manager that the request for additional funding of the business with an overdraft is reasonable, the business has been asked to draw up a cash flow forecast for the first 7 months of operations from June to December.

- Use Lotus 1-2-3 to create the cash flow table that the bank manager wants to see before granting the overdraft provision requested. The cash flow table will also need to show size of the overdraft required.
- You should produce not only the print of the table as seen on the screen, but also a print showing the formulae used, in case the bank manager questions the derivation of the figures.

In October the business finds that it is proceeding very much as had been planned and that advance orders suggest that sales are likely to rise to 150 from January, falling to 130 from April. This is extremely encouraging but leaves the business with the problem of how it is going to be able to satisfy demand.

Production capacity of 120 ovens a month has been sufficient to cope with demand thus far, but...

Overtime working, which will inevitably increase labour costs, seems to be called for and the business is to consider how this can be organised. The directors have already talked to staff and sufficient staff have said they would be willing to work overtime.

It is estimated that when production rises above 120 per month each microwave will add £40 to labour costs. Also, while the factory is working overtime, overheads will rise to £5,800 per month. New machinery and maintenance costs of £12,000 will have to be paid for in April.

- Use your existing spreadsheet model as a starting point and modify accordingly. Extend the cash budget to June investigating some of the possibilities. You may assume that only labour costs and additional overheads will be affected by the overtime working, and you should remember that selling microwaves that have not yet been produced is not an acceptable means of improving cash flow.

In order that you have a record of the consequences of the alternative strategies you have investigated, you should print copies of the spreadsheets with sub-headings which indicate what strategy you were examining.

—— 10.13 Council house survey ——

On examination of the sample spreadsheet in **Screen dump 10.11**, it should be evident what is required from the survey in terms of the initial data.

The aim is to show in graphical form the types of housing stock that exist within this fictitious borough council and the number of people living in the houses.

From the spreadsheet you are to extract a number of bar graphs (or pie charts) showing the distribution of the total housing among the various groups and the number of occupants in each type of accommodation. You will be able to produce a large number of useful charts from such figures.

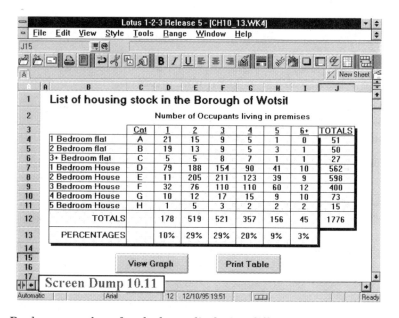

Screen Dump 10.11

Produce a number of such charts displaying different aspects of data, so that someone else can understand the data quickly and easily without having to read through the table.

When setting up a bar chart or pie chart, one of the problems you will soon face is avoiding too much congestion on the screen.

As a finishing touch, create two macros, one to print the table and the other to view the graph. Assign these two macros to buttons in order to simplify the process for a user.

APPENDIX:
SmartIcons

A SmartIcon is a small picture made up of tiny dots, called pixels. Linked to each of the images is a macro which is activated when you click your mouse on the SmartIcon.

This appendix serves as a quick reference guide to the SmartIcons available with Lotus 1-2-3. The icons that appear can be altered to suit your own requirements and moved around the spreadsheet. The size of the SmartIcons can also be altered.

—— Changing the SmartIcons ——

- To alter the appearance of your SmartIcons and which ones you want to appear, click on Tools and then click on SmartIcons. **Screen dump A.1** shows the dialogue box that appears.

The SmartIcon control dialogue box shows a list of two sets of SmartIcons. The Available icons box lists all SmartIcons available with Lotus 1-2-3. The list of SmartIcons to the right of this has been organised into sets of SmartIcons that you can have displayed and available on any spreadsheet. Down the right side of the dialogue box appear some buttons.

The Position box allows you the choice of where the icons are to appear on the spreadsheet; top, bottom, left, right or floating. When they are floating, you can move the row of SmartIcons up and down your spreadsheet with your mouse.

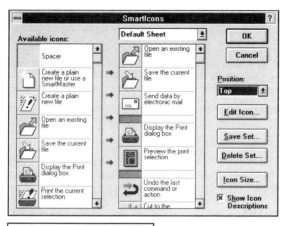

Screen Dump A.1

Editing or creating your own SmartIcons

The Edit Icon allows you to create your own SmartIcon or to modify an existing one. If you observe **Screen dump A.2**, you will see how this works.

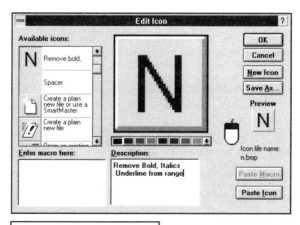

Screen Dump A.2

You can either create a new SmartIcon by clicking on the <u>N</u>ew Icon button, or click on an available icon to edit it. The available icons box allows you to select one to edit. Many of the SmartIcons cannot be edited because they form an integral part of the Lotus 1-2-3 package. If you do select one of these, the program allows you to create a copy of the SmartIcon in the centre box for editing. When the image appears, you can use your mouse to add pixels to the image or remove existing ones. By clicking on the colour pallet below the SmartIcon image, you can add colour to your design.

The <u>E</u>nter macro here: box allows you either to paste a macro recorded in your Clipboard or write one of your own. To paste a macro to this box, you would click on the Paste Macro button.

The <u>D</u>escription is what will appear alongside the SmartIcon in the main SmartIcon dialogue box when it is activated.

Creating your own set of SmartIcons

This facility allows you to tailor your own set of SmartIcons to appear on your spreadsheet. You can make your own combination of Smart-Icons either from the list of available ones or by creating your own.

• To create your own set, click on the <u>S</u>ave Set button on the main SmartIcon dialogue box.

A new dialogue box will appear allowing you to create a new set. **Screen dump A.3** shows such a dialogue box.

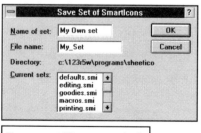

The Name of set: gives the set a name so that it can be selected from the main SmartIcon dialogue box as the set you require on your screen. The File name: is needed so that Lotus 1-2-3 can save the set for future reference. Once this has been done, you should click on the **OK** button to start creating the set.

To remove SmartIcons from the set, use the mouse to click on the SmartIcon, hold the right button of the mouse down, and drag the image out of the list.

To add SmartIcons, drag and drop a SmartIcon from the available list to your new set box. As SmartIcons are added to your list, the list of available SmartIcons will remain intact.

Screen dump A.4 shows the way in which SmartIcons are added to the list by the drag and drop method.

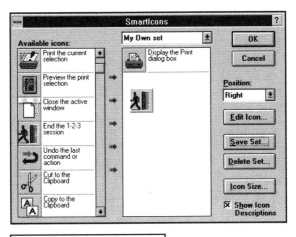

Screen Dump A.4

Once the new set has been added to the existing sets, you can choose it to be the SmartIcons that by default appear on your screen. Remember that the screen will only display a limited number at any one time.

SmartIcon reference

All the Screen dumps that follow serves as a reference to assist you
identifying what each SmartIcon can do.

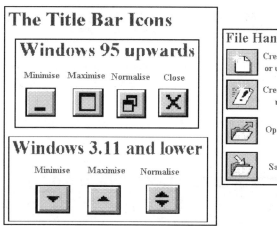

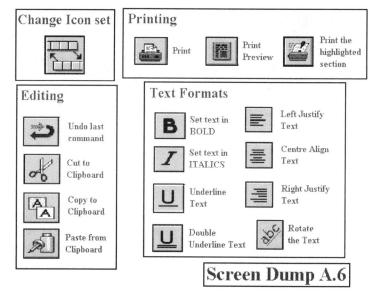

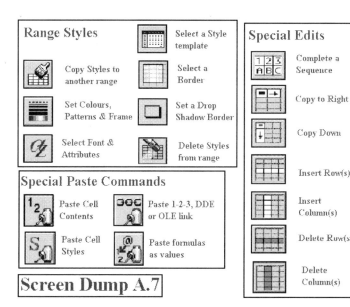

Range Styles

Select a Style template

Copy Styles to another range

Select a Border

Set Colours, Patterns & Frame

Set a Drop Shadow Border

Select Font & Attributes

Delete Styles from range

Special Paste Commands

Paste Cell Contents

Paste 1-2-3, DDE or OLE link

Paste Cell Styles

Paste formulas as values

Special Edits

Complete a Sequence

Copy to Right

Copy Down

Insert Row(s)

Insert Column(s)

Delete Row(s)

Delete Column(s)

Screen Dump A.7

Advanced Print Commands

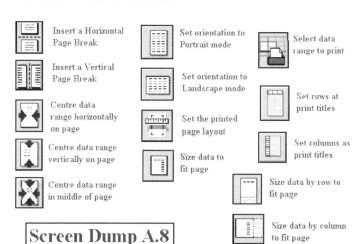

Insert a Horizontal Page Break

Set orientation to Portrait mode

Select data range to print

Insert a Vertical Page Break

Set orientation to Landscape mode

Centre data range horizontally on page

Set the printed page layout

Set rows at print titles

Centre data range vertically on page

Size data to fit page

Set columns as print titles

Centre data range in middle of page

Size data by row to fit page

Size data by column to fit page

Screen Dump A.8

Lotus Goodies

Create an
Approach Form

Create an
Approach Report

Create an Approach
Dynamic Crosstab

Draw a Chart
with a data range

Draw a Map

Copy a Range
Style

Versions and
Scenarios

Spell Check

Size columns
for widest fit

Complete a
sequence in a
range

Select Style
Template

Show or Hide
data

Create a
Query table

Cross tabulate
values from a
table

Audit cells

Screen Dump A.9

Finding things

Find
formulas

Find formula
precedents

Find cell
dependents

Find links to
1-2-3 files

Find DDE
Links

Finding cells

Find next cell DOWN
adjoining a blank

Find next cell RIGHT
adjoining a blank

Find next cell UP
adjoining a blank

Find next cell LEFT
adjoining a blank

Go To ..

.. first cell in
next range

.. first cell in
previous range

.. next sheet
or page

.. last sheet
or page

Screen Dump A.10

RECALCULATION

Visual
effects

Zoom IN

Zoom OUT

Linking with other programs

 Embed data in the worksheet

 Start Lotus Organiser

 Start Ami Pro

 Start Lotus Notes

 Start Approach

 Start cc:Mail

 Start Freelance Graphics

 Start ScreenCam

 Start Improv

 Start SmartPics

 Start Lotus Dialog Editor

Start File Manager

Ranges

 Insert a Range

 Delete a Range

 Create and Delete Range names

 The MSDOS prompt

Screen Dump A.11

Macro Commands

 Draw a Macro button

 Select a Macro Command

 Run a Macro

 Turn Step mode on or off

 Turn Macro Recording ON

 Show or hide transcript window

 Turn Macro Recording OFF

 Start the Macro translator

Windows Navigation

 Close active Window

 Arrange open windows side by side

 Arrange open diagonally (Cascade)

 Go to Top left cell

 Find bottom right cell of active area

Screen Dump A.12

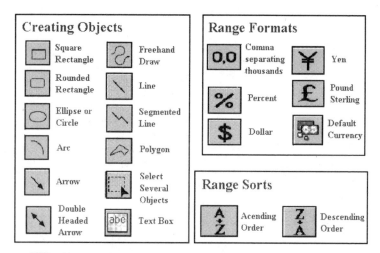

Creating Objects

	Square Rectangle		Freehand Draw
	Rounded Rectangle		Line
	Ellipse or Circle		Segmented Line
	Arc		Polygon
	Arrow		Select Several Objects
	Double Headed Arrow	abc	Text Box

Range Formats

0,0	Comma separating thousands	¥	Yen
%	Percent	£	Pound Sterling
$	Dollar		Default Currency

Range Sorts

A↓Z	Acending Order	Z↓A	Descending Order

Screen Dump A.13

GLOSSARY

Abort   The action of stopping the execution of a program while it is still running. If you are in the middle of updating a record, for example, you may need to abort to avoid a serious error. In Lotus 1-2-3 this is usually done by pressing the **Esc** key.

Absolute cell address   This is a cell reference in a formula, prefixed with a $ (dollar), sign that fixes a cell reference when the formula is copied.

Access   Referring to data stored in a file. For example, disk access is needed if a formerly saved Spreadsheet file is to be opened and subsequently amended.

Algorithm   A series of instructions set up in logical order and designed to perform an activity such as sorting stock records into stock number order. The algorithm will be capable of being converted into a computer program.

Amend   Changing the contents of a file, whether a spreadsheet file or a database file. If you need to access a file and subsequently change its contents, then you are said to have amended the file.

Analyst   A person who has the job of analysing various activities, for example, systems analyst, database analyst, cost analyst. With respect to the systems analyst, such people are often concerned with analysing computer-based information systems or manual systems with the view of computerising them. The use of spreadsheet may be one of many applications an analyst will consider.

Annotating   The process of creating and editing objects such as polygons, text boxes and rectangles. Such annotated objects can be created in a chart and subsequently added to spreadsheets and graphs.

Append   Adding a record to a file, such as adding a new customer to a database.

Application   A specific use to which a computer is put, for example, spreadsheet, payroll, sales, job costing. Such applications are often performed on a computer by a software package, or part of an integrated software package.

At (@) functions   Special addition functions that will perform a range of arithmetic operations. For example, @SUM(range) adds all numbers in the specified range. Lotus has a large number of such functions, covering many specialist areas as well as the more general ones.

Background printing   A process whereby the computer prints a document while continuing to allow an operator to use the computer or computer terminal to process data.

Backing storage   Often referred to as secondary storage, it allows data to be stored on media such as disks for long-term storage purposes, i.e. off-line data storage.

Backup   A process of copying all data from one source to another for safekeeping. This option is offered by Lotus 1-2-3 when you attempt to save a file with that name.

Bar code   Often found on retail products, this is a set of pre-printed vertical bars holding information about the product, such as where it was made, who made it, its weight or its size. Computers can read these codes quickly using a bar code reader. Such details can, for example, help computers determine a price for the product by accessing a related record in a database.

Batch processing The processing of grouping transactions together and then processing them all at once. For example, a firm may choose to enter all invoice details sent to it by suppliers at pre-determined times in the week, rather than entering them up as and when they arrive.

Bootstrap A small program built into the computer that instructs the system about how to set itself up when switched on. Part of the bootstrap is often held on disks, which are also needed when a machine is switched on.

Borders These are the letter and number indicators around the spreadsheet area, letters along the top and numbers down the left side, that help identify cell locations. Lotus 1-2-3 allows you to remove them from the screen.

Bubble jet printer A type of non-impact printer. Such printers offer a cheap and high quality method of printing.

Buffer A part of memory used as a temporary store to hold data from an input device. For example, most printers have a buffer memory for storing data prior to printing it. Also, keyboards often hold at least one line of data before it is sent to the computer's processor.

Bug An error in a program.

Bus A means of communication channel which data travel along. Such channels consist of a control bus, data bus, address bus and peripheral bus.

Button A small button-like object on the screen that, when activated with a mouse, starts a macro running.

Byte A measure of computer memory, normally containing 8 single bits. Each byte often represents a single character. 1024 of these bytes is referred to as a Kilobyte.

Cache memory A form of buffer memory that works at high speed and is capable of keeping up with a computer's main central processor. It acts as a buffer between the central processor and the slower main memory. Because the central processor is not delayed by memory access, processing is speeded up. The operator will load segments of programs into cache memory from disks.

Card reader An input device that reads data from cards. The data on such cards can be in magnetic form or can be simply holes punched into the cards.

Carriage return A single character sent to the computer by pressing the **Return** or **Enter** key on the keyboard. Such carriage returns are often used to release data from the keyboard buffer to the computer's processor.

Cascading windows This shows different windows one behind the other. Cascading spreadsheets will give the image of spreadsheets piled up. You will have to have more than one spreadsheet open at any time to get the benefit of this or work with multiple sheets in a spreadsheet.

CD ROM An acronym for Compact Disk Read Only Memory. These are popular high density disk-storage devices which can be read by computers.

Cell pointer Indicates which cell will be next for data input.

Central processing unit Often referred to as the processor or microprocessor, and is the main unit of any computer system. The processor accepts its data from input devices, processes the data and sends it to output devices such as screens and printers or to a disk for saving.

Character A single element in coded form for the processor, such as a letter or a single number digit. Such characters are normally 8 bits, or one byte, long.

Clipboard A part of computer memory that can store information away from the main processing. It is well used in the Lotus package for storing data and then pasting it back to the spreadsheet later.

Clock A processor contains an electronic pulse generator that is used to transmit synchronised pulses to different parts of the computer for the interpretation and execution of instructions. The synchronisation is set at a speed that determines the computer's CLOCK SPEED. Such clock speeds are measured in Megahertz (MHz). The faster the clock speed, the faster the internal processing speed of the computer. For most business applications, the access time to disks is more important to processing speed than the clock speed.

COM Computer Output on Microfilm. A form of computer output that offers an effective form of long-term data storage that is both compact and durable. Such output is especially useful as a means of archiving data.

Command An instruction to the computer to perform a given task.

Computer Aided Design (CAD) The use of a computer with graphics software to design through electronic drawing. Main applications areas are in the fields of engineering drawing, product design, fashion design and technical drawing.

Computer bureau A commercial enterprise offering computing services to organisations. Many firms still use computer bureaux to manage their payrolls. Some computer bureaux can offer on-line services by installing a terminal into the firm and thereby offering computing time on a time-sharing basis.

Control Unit That part of the computer's Central Processing Unit or micro processor which controls the movements of data within it.

Correlation A statistical term used to express whether there is a relationship between two variables. For example, between rainfall and temperature. Lotus 1-2-3 has the facility to calculate whether such correlation exists and can show such correlation graphically via a scatter graph.

Corruption A term used to refer to the loss, or corruption, of data. Data corruption is a particular problem when it occurs on a disk. Such corruption can often render data on a disk useless, hence the importance of regular backing-up of data.

Criteria This sets out the conditions against which records are extracted or deleted from a database. A criteria table has to be set up on Lotus for this facility to work.

Cursor A small image such as a block or dash on the screen to indicate where data will be entered from the keyboard.

Customising A process of altering a package or environment to suit a particular application. For example, you can set up a set of SmartIcons especially for a specific spreadsheet application.

Daisy wheel printer A type of impact printer that prints by striking character images on carbonated ribbon. The characters appear on the ends of spokes on a small wheel. The results on paper are of a high quality but print style is limited to whatever characters are on the wheel. Particularly good for letter or report writing.

Data An element that needs processing to form the basis of information. It can take the form of an electronic pulse, a magnetic particle, a hole in a piece of paper, a particle of light or any other physical form that can be represented in one of two states. The pattern of this data that will be processed by the computer.

Data capture The way in which data is captured, collected or input for processing. Methods of data capture can vary from entering data by bar code readers reading bar codes to scanners, Optical Character Recognition, and source documents requiring keying in. The methods of direct input to the computer are increasing, as data capture is often the most time-consuming and error-prone part of general data-processing operations.

Database The collection, in structured form, of all data representing the basis of information for an organisation's business applications. Lotus allows a database structure to be set up on the spreadsheet as well as having direct links with database packages.

Database Management System (DBMS) Software that manages computerised databases such as updating, creating and interrogating. Such software also manages the efficiency of data storage, data security and integrity.

DataLens driver A program that Lotus 1-2-3 uses to access data in external database tables. There are different datalens drivers for each database package.

Dedicated computer A computer system set up to perform one specific task or set of tasks. For example, a cash dispenser or an electronic cash till.

Default When offering a choice to users through software, a default value is assumed if no choice is made. For example, when a spreadsheet file is saved, the default extension is .WK4. Such defaults can be changed when they occur.

Diagnostic routine A program used to detect errors in either existing software or hardware. Many diagnostic routines will operate in a way that does not interfere with normal operations and is not apparent to a user.

Dialogue boxes   These appear during various Lotus 1-2-3 activities and require an operator to enter parameters in order carry out an operation.

DIP (Dual Inline Package)   An integrated circuit having two rows of connector pins. Most printers have DIP switches which allow settings to be altered in such a way that the connections to the printer are made compatible with both a computer's hardware and software.

Disk drive   A peripheral device for storing data generated by the computer's processor and for retrieving data by the processor. Disk drives can contain either floppy disks or hard disks.

DOS (Disk Operating System)   Part of the software that is contained on disk, which is loaded into computer memory and is used to operate the computer system.

Down time   The amount of time a computer is not functioning.

Download   The process of loading a program into computer memory.

Drag and drop   An object or range of cells can be moved around the spreadsheet with the aid of a mouse dragging it to a new location. When the mouse button is released, the object or range is dropped into a new location.

Driver   A part of the operating system software that is used to control certain peripheral devices.

Duplex   A communications concept that allows simultaneous data transmission down a line in both directions

EFTPOS   Electronic Funds Transfer at Point Of Sale. This allows funds to be transferred from a customer's account to a trader's account as and when a transaction takes place, thereby avoiding cash transfer.

Electronic mail (e-mail)   A process of electronically transmitting messages and mail between computers. Such mail can be stored for future reference.

EPOS   Electronic Point of Sale such as check-out systems in supermarkets that can scan bar codes and price products. Many such terminals can now perform database activities.

Exception reporting   A process of reporting any circumstances that are unusual or not normally permitted, such as reporting large customer orders or reporting low stock levels on certain items of stock.

Expert system   Software orientated, it enables a computer to diagnose problems, given the symptoms. Such expert systems often contain information about past events and calculate likely causes of problems through statistical analysis.

Facsimile (FAX)   A common method of transporting files and documents across a telephone line. Such a document is converted, using special hardware, into a format that can be transmitted across a line and then translated back by similar hardware at the other end.

Fibre optics   A cabling medium for transmitting data. As an alternative form to coaxial cable, it transmits data via light pulses and allows a much greater and more reliable capacity than coaxial cable.

Field   An element of a record that is a collection of characters such as that which makes up a customer name or stock number.

File   A collection of records that are related in some way. A stock file, for example, may be a collection of stock records.

File protection   A method of protecting files from corruption or accidental erasure. A common way of protecting a file is to write protect it, which means files can be read but not written to.

Firmware   Software that is set on read only memory and can be easily replaced in the computer. It offers a reliable source of software and is particularly useful when an application is often used.

Floppy disk   A backup medium used to store data. Such disks require a disk drive in order for the computer to read from them and write to them.

Flowchart   A diagrammatic way of showing functions and sequences of events within a system or sub-system. Flowcharts can take different forms, such as program flowcharts depicting the way a program runs, or systems flowcharts showing the way a system works.

Form feed   A process whereby a printer feeds a sheet of paper through the printer. This is often used to align continuous paper on a printer to the top of the next sheet.

Format   The way data is structured on disk, paper or screens. With respect to disks, it is important that new disks are formatted in a way that is compatible with the computer system before they can be used.

Fourth Generation Languages (4GL)   A programming language that has a high-level structure allowing programming to be done by English-style statements. Such 4GLs have normally been tailored for certain applications, such as databases.

Front-end processors   A method whereby some processing on a large computer system is done by terminals or microcomputers, such as screen layouts, communications transmission, editing, data validation and verification.

Function   A general term used to identify a specific group of related tasks, such as the accounting function, stock-control function or payroll function.

General purpose computer   A computer that can be adapted to a wide range of applications by loading the appropriate software.

Generation of files   Often referred to as the grandfather-father-son principle, creates a generation of backed up files. With the cost of storage being relatively cheap, it is often prudent to keep many generations of backed up files.

Grid lines   Horizontal and vertical lines that show each individual cell on a spreadsheet.

Group mode   This sets all pages in a spreadsheet to be styled in the same manner. When a set of pages, or sheets, are grouped, the alteration of style in any one of them becomes common to all.

Hacking   The attempt to gain unauthorised access to computerised information, for example, by trying to use modem equipment to gain access to private information held on computer databases.

Half duplex   A process of data transmission whereby data can be sent in both directions down a communication line, but NOT simultaneously.

Handshaking   A process whereby both computer and peripheral tell each other that data transmission is ready to commence. A printer requires this because it is normally unable to print data as fast as it can receive it, so the principle of handshaking ensures data is sent down as and when the printer is ready, thereby preventing loss of data.

Hard copy   Printed output from a computer.

Hard disk   This is the disk storage unit contained within a computer. Hard disks have the ability to store very large amounts of data.

Hardware   The physical attributes of any computer system.

High-level language   A programming language that is constructed of statements containing English-style words. Such high-level languages vary in type and sophistication. Examples are COBOL, Basic, Pascal, C, Fortran and Modula-2.

Housekeeping   A term used to describe the practice of not keeping unwanted information on disks and tapes. Good housekeeping will prevent disks from becoming cluttered, speed up processing and lessen the chance of filling up a disk unnecessarily.

IBM   The abbreviated trade name for International Business Machines.

ICL   The abbreviated trade name for International Computers Limited.

Icon   A pictorial representation of programs, document file and options available for executing or processing. With respect to Lotus 1-2-3, these appear down the right of the screen and are often used as an alternative to activating menu command sequences.

Image processing   The process of transmitting pictures and images in digitised form.

Impact printers   A category of printer that creates images on paper by physically hitting the paper; such as matrix or daisy wheel printers.

Ink jet printers   Non-impact printers. Such printers offer a cheap and high-quality source of printed output.
Input   The process of entering data, either manually or electronically, into a computer.
Installing   The process of placing software on to a computer for the first time and making sure it works within the computer environment.
Integer   A whole number.
Interface   A general term used to describe the processing of data between two systems or sub-systems. For example, a disk interface refers to the process of transferring data from processor to disk and back. Such interfaces are collections of both hardware and software.
Job   In a computing context, this refers to either routines or applications being run on a computer system at any one point in time.
Job costing   The process of attributing costs against a specific job. In accounting terms, this could be a specific contract or the manufacture of a particular product.
Justification   A technique where a block of text is set with text formatted against left- and right-hand margins. Lotus 1-2-3 has the facility to left and right justify text in a cell as well as justify a block of text or text in a text object.
Key field   A field within a record that identifies the record itself and is used to access the record.
Keyboard   One of the most commonly used forms of input devices.
Kilobyte (K)   Used to measure data quantity. It represents 1024 bytes of data.
Kimball tag   Either pre-punched or magnetised card containing information about an item. Often seen in retail outlets, these are used as a storage medium that can hold details about a product. An appropriate computer input device can then read them.
Landscape printing   This turns a spreadsheet sideways when printing. It is particularly useful when a spreadsheet is wide and occupies only a few rows.
Laser printer   A type of non-impact printer giving high-quality printed output. Its technology is similar to that of a photocopier.
Legend   An object of text combined with images to explain what variables are represented on a chart.
Line printer   Low quality, very high speed printers that print complete lines at a time.
Local Area Network (LAN)   A system that connects a number of microcomputers together so that they can share common resources such as a database or printer. While resources can be shared, each computer on a network is still able to act independently of the others.
Logging in   A method of getting access to a computer's information. Designed for security, the process of logging in requires an operator to enter identification and, normally, an associated password.
Logging out   Signing off a system. This should be done whenever an operator has finished work on a computer.
Macro   A stored sequence of commands that can all be activated in their sequence with just one action.
Magnetic disks   A storage medium for data which fits into a disk drive. There are many different types of disk suitable for different types of application and computer systems.
Magnetic Ink Character Recognition (MICR)   Typically used by banks, magnetic ink characters are read by the computer as a way of inputting data to the computer. Magnetic characters typically appear on the bottom of cheques and are used to assist banks in processing a large volume of cheques.
Magnetic tape   A form of backing store medium that is mounted on to tape drives and can store data serially. Magnetic tapes offer an effective and cheap form of backup storage for systems with a large amount of data. They are also used for storing programs that are subsequently loaded into computer memory.
Mainframe computer   An exceptionally large computer often capable of supporting many hundreds of computer terminals, microcomputers, storage units, printers and other peripherals. Mainframe computers are used as large central processors

supporting remote systems by data communication links across long distances.

Management Information System (MIS)   Often operated in conjunction with other data processing activities, it is used to extract a whole series of reports. With most MIS packages, users are able to identify their own information needs and extract reports to meet them.

Matrix printer   An impact printer that creates an image on paper through a dot pattern on a matrix. Such matrix printers are effective for printing graphics as well as near-letter-quality text at low cost. Such printers are often quite adequate for most smaller businesses using computers for accounts, word processing and management information.

Megabyte (MByte)   A measure of data memory. One megabyte is made up of 1024 bytes. Typically, a single letter of the alphabet will be stored by a computer as one byte.

Menu   A list of options to choose from. With Lotus 1-2-3, these menus are activated with the / key for the general menus and the : (colon) for the WYSIWYG menu structure.

Merge   Combining two related files (normally having the same structure, if they are data files) to create one larger file.

Microprocessor   The more common description for the processing unit of a microcomputer.

Minicomputer   Similar to a mainframe computer but on a smaller scale. The distinction between a mainframe and minicomputer is not an obvious one, but minicomputers are often multi-user/tasking machines that can support many peripherals (about 100) on either a local or distributed processing basis.

Mode indicator   An indicator on the spreadsheet that informs the operator about the status the spreadsheet is in. For example, READY indicates the spreadsheet is waiting for input while WAIT indicates the computer is busy.

Modulator/Demodulator (MODEM)   A device for sending and receiving signals down a telephone line, thereby allowing data communication between computer devices. Modems will be needed at both ends of a line for data communications to work.

Mouse   An input device that interacts with the screen. It moves the image of an arrow or bar around the screen and is used to select options when the mouse button is clicked.

MSDOS   The abbreviated trade name for MicroSoft Disk Operating System.

Multiplexer   A communications device that receives data from a number of computer devices and then sends such data down ONE telephone line. There will be a slowing down in data communications transmission from each device as more of them transmit data, but such devices can reduce the costs of data communications quite considerably.

Network   This is a computer configuration where computers, and their devices, are linked together so that they can share data and resources such as hard disks and printers.

Object   An item that can appear in the form of a shape or box on a spreadsheet and be edited, deleted or moved around the spreadsheet. A graph, for example, is a collection of such objects.

Off-line   A general term referring to data or part of a computer system being inaccessible. In other words, data on a disk which is not in the computer disk drive is said to be off-line.

Off-line data processing   A process of working on data away from the main computer system or on, say, a microcomputer, before interacting with the main system. With the cost and power of microcomputers, it often makes sense to prepare data, such as invoices, off-line and then batch-process the work to a mainframe or minicomputer later. Off-line processing can also involve many manual operations as preparation and validation of data before computerised (On-line) processing.

Operating System   Software that is used to operate the computer and its peripherals.

Operator   A term used to describe a person who operates a computer. This is different from a person who programs a computer, a computer programmer.

Optical character reader A computer input device that recognises characters, usually in typed form; can be a considerable labour saving device when text that has already been typed needs to be entered to the computer.

Output range A part of the spreadsheet that Lotus can place data from a database subject to defined criteria.

Parallel running A process of running two systems together, typically a computer system and a manual system. This may be a necessary prerequisite to automating a manual process with computers. Such parallel processing will help to detect any errors or bugs in the new system. Such parallel running should be temporary in most cases.

Password A way of ensuring that only authorised personnel have access to parts of a system. Passwords are only effective if they are kept secret from everyone excluding authorised persons. Passwords are set up in a way that ensures different people have access to different parts of the system.

Paste This refers to the process of placing what is stored into computer memory on to the spreadsheet.

Payroll The function of paying employees. Computers are useful for this.

Peripheral device Input, output and storage devices of a computer that constitute part of a system hardware.

Portrait An orientation for printing documents. This tends to be the default print orientation where printing is done top across the shortest dimension of the paper.

POS Point-of-sale.

Prestel A public database service offered by British Telecom.

Protocol Communications protocol is a standard of data communications that tries to ensure compatibility in the way data is communicated across lines.

Random file A file organisation principle that allows the computer to access any record directly without having to read all records preceding it sequentially. Naturally, such files are normally stored on disk medium.

RAM (Random Access Memory) A part of the computer's memory that is internal. Such memory is blank until the computer is switched on. It is needed in order to run applications.

Range A block of cells referenced by the top left and bottom right cells to give a rectangular block.

Read/write heads A device contained within a disk drive or tape drive that either reads data into the computer or writes data on to a storage medium from the computer.

Real-time processing A concept of ensuring files and databases are updated by transactions as the transaction occurs. To achieve real-time processing, procedures on operating a computer system are just as important as having the hardware and software capabilities to do it.

Record An element of a database used to store attributes about, for example, a person, item of stock or invoice details.

Relative cell address When a formula is copied from a cell or range of cells to another location, any formula that contains cell references will alter relative to their new position in the spreadsheet. You can prevent this by using the $ (dollar) sign to make a cell reference absolute.

Remote Job Entry (RJE) This is the process of entering data to computer where the entry is geographically separate from the central processing unit. RJE is typified by a Remote Terminal being linked by modem to mainframe or minicomputer.

Report generator A part of a software package that allows a user to design their own reports based on their information needs. It allows much greater freedom on the way a user can extract available data from the system.

ROM (Read Only Memory) A part of the memory in a computer used to store programs in a permanent way. Part of a computer's operating system (e.g. BIOS) is stored here. Some systems will also have applications' software built into ROM.

Root directory In any hierarchical directory structure, there will be a starting point from which all sub-directories begin. This starting point is referred to as the root directory.

Run   The execution of a program.

Scheduling   A process of determining the order in which jobs are performed or executed. Such activities can be carried out automatically or by operating, with priorities being set on certain jobs. Important when working on networks systems.

Scrolling   A process of running text up the screen when you want to view data past the bottom of the screen. The alternative to scrolling is to clear a screen in such a way that one complete screen at a time is viewed. Scroll bars are available on the Lotus package for this purpose.

Search and replace   A technique of replacing a word or set of words in a piece of text with another word or set of words available in word-processing applications and in Lotus 1-2-3.

Sequential access   A file-reading method whereby data is read in a defined sequence. With magnetic tape, the order of sequential access is the order in which it was saved. Programs are also read sequentially on whatever medium they are stored. Some files support an index which allows files to be read in different sequences.

Sequential file   A file where data is stored physically in the order in which it is generated.

Silicon chip   A small piece of silicon-based material used to hold computer circuits to form a microprocessor. New technology has allowed many thousands of transistors and diodes to be stored on one single chip.

Simplex transmission   A method of data communication where transmission of data can be made in ONE DIRECTION ONLY.

SmartIcon   A pictorial representation of programs, document file and options available for executing or processing. In Lotus 1-2-3, these appear down the right of the screen and are often used as an alternative to activating menu command sequences.

Soft copy   A term used for screen output.

Software   All computer programs, from operating system to applications software.

Sort   A data processing term used when rearranging files into a different order.

Source code   The program as written by a computer programmer before it is compiled to form object code. High level languages, for example, are first written in source code, and the computer uses a compiler to convert this source into something it can run from.

Spool   Often referred to as a file awaiting printing. When outputting data, you are often given the option of spool output, which means output is to file for future processing or printing.

Stand-alone system   A computer that is capable of working in isolation from any other system. Most microcomputers are stand-alone systems.

Status   A signal indicating whether a system is active or not.

Storage capacity   A way of measuring the amount of data that can be stored. Storage capacity is normally measured in Kilobyte (K).

Sub-directory   This is a part of the directory that branches from another directory. Lotus 1-2-3 is normally stored in a series of sub-directories on your hard disk. Different sub-directories are used for different file types.

Suite   A set of inter-related programs. A term often used instead of package.

Systems analysis   The job of analysing systems both manual and computerised with the view of implementing new systems or modifying existing ones. The job of a systems analyst will often include implementing systems, a role that requires communications and business management skills as much as computing ones.

Telecommunication   Refers to the general concept of sending data from one device to another down a telephone line.

Teleprocessing   The use of telecommunications in order to achieve on-line data processing. In other words, to interact with a database from a remote distance, using transmission lines and a terminal.

Template   This is a spreadsheet that has the basic structure and outline in place, but not the precise data. For example, an invoice template would contain the outline of the invoice requiring you to complete the customer details and details about the goods sent to the customer. Lotus 1-2-3 comes with such templates. There are also a few templates contained in the disk pack version of this book.

Test data Data generated and specifically used for testing systems and their software; may have to be created when being used to test a new system or set of software.

Tiling windows The method of displaying a number of windows screens at the same time by splitting the screen into sections.

Time sharing A technique where a processor shares its time among more than one user. Some operating systems have time sharing built in as required to allow users to use a system.

Transaction data Any data generated from the result of a transaction such as a sale or purchase or stock movement. Such transaction data will often be stored as a record per transaction in a set of transaction files and will be used to update master files.

Turnkey system A system supplied that simply means switching on and starting. Such systems are normally supplied by outside agencies or consultancy services.

Underscore Underlining of text and numbers.

Undo This is a technique of reversing the most recent command carried out. Lotus 1-2-3 stores the sequence of commands and is able to perform this reversal.

Updating The process of altering a spreadsheet or database to more accurately reflect a current situation, such as entering an address that has been altered.

User-friendly A term often associated with the way software guides a user through processes when operating a computer application package.

Utility program A program that can be used to manage files or perform activities outside the normal scope of running a program, such as file backup, retrieving lost files and deleting unwanted files.

Validate A process of checking whether data conforms to expected input such as valid date, or ensuring alphabetic characters are not entered when the computer expects a number.

Verification A way of confirming with an operator that data input is complete and correct, or a certain action is what is required (the 'ARE YOU SURE?' message).

Vision Display Unit (VDU) The screen that displays text and graphic output as soft copy.

Virtual storage This is a technique whereby the computer uses backing store, usually disk, as part of the processing area in addition to that of internal memory. In this way it can use very large programs that are normally beyond the memory capabilities of the machine it is running on. An example is the way in which only a small part of the Lotus software is loaded into memory at any one time.

Winchester drive A storage device that holds a hard disk. The hard disk is non-removable and offers high storage density and capacity and is generally very reliable.

Window A method of sectioning the VDU in such a way that an operator can see different parts of a spreadsheet or run and see different applications at the same time.

Word processing An application that involves processing words and spending time perfecting format, spelling and so on, before producing hard copy. Word processors have largely replaced typewriters.

WYSIWYG An acronym for What You See Is What You Get. In Lotus, the WYSIWYG features are activated using the : (colon) and give a menu structure of their own. The purpose of WYSIWYG is to give spreadsheets and graphs improved presentation and take advantage of graphic screens and printers.

Zoom A technique of increasing the size of an image on screen. It has the appearance of zooming in on a document. The term is also used for doing the reverse of this i.e. zooming out.

INDEX